CONCEIVE IT, BELIEVE IT, AND ACHIEVE IT!

That's the essence of Willie Jolley's recipe for success. Every day, people across the country gain inspiration from his one-minute radio show, "The Magnificent Motivational Minute." Now, everyone everywhere can be inspired and motivated by his stories, poems, anecdotes, songs and affirming lessons. They will help you get more out of life and put more into life. Ideas that will help you live your dreams. Learn how to:

- Tap into the power of each minute!
- Rediscover the dreams that are buried within you!
- Stay away from "The DreamBusters"!
- Take control of your life and design your future!
- Develop a positive and productive mental attitude!
- Overcome obstacles and rise above circumstances!
- Make your dreams a reality!
- Live Life to the Fullest and Enjoy Every Minute!

In a time of minute rice, instant coffee, fast food, quick cash and speedy phone loans, we are now happy to present "Minute Motivation." Busy people have little, or no, time to spare. So now is the time to change your life. Remember it's not how much time you have, but what you do with the time you've got! It only takes a minute to change your life! Do it now!

It Only Takes A Minute To Change Your Life!

Willie Jolley

St. Martin's Paperbacks

Quotes from Benjamin Mays on pp. 2 and 11 are being reprinted with permission from *Quotable Quotes* © 1983 by Dr. Benjamin Mays, published by Vantage Press.

Lyrics for "It Only Takes a Minute" copyright © 1995 Ninatom Music (ASCAP), Rojo Grande Music (ASCAP). All rights reserved. Used by permission.

Lyrics for "Sky Is the Limit" copyright © 1996 Ninatom Music (ASCAP), Rojo Grande Music (ASCAP), Paul Minor Music (BMI). All rights reserved. Used by permission.

Lyrics for "Midnight Phoenix" by Diane Elizabeth Kenney, from the play "Skegee" by Deborah Sims-Wood.

IT ONLY TAKES A MINUTE TO CHANGE YOUR LIFE

ISBN: 0-312-96110-3

Printed in the United States of America

10 9

Dedication

This book is dedicated to my wife, Dee, who is not only my wife but also my best friend, and, most of all, my queen, whose love, support, and hard work made this book a reality. To my children, William and LaToya, for their love and support. To my mother, Catherine B. Jolley, for her unending love, support, and faith in me. To David Metcalf, for his assistance in getting this book started. To Rhonda Davis Smith and Darlene Bryant, for their help and high standards as readers. Finally, this book is dedicated to the memory of my mother-in-law, Lillie Mae Taylor, who passed while I was writing this book yet who continued to love, encourage, inspire, and motivate me up until her death and continues to do so even today. I Love You Always!

WILLIE JOLLEY

Contents

Foreword
by Les Brown

I first met Willie Jolley during an appearance I made at Howard University in Washington, D.C. As usual, at the end of my presentation, I took a few minutes for questions from the audience. A young man stepped up to the microphone and said just a few words. I knew then that there was something special about Willie Jolley and I asked him to stick around after the program so we could have a few words together. He promised he would.

This particular evening, I was swamped with people wanting interviews and autographs and my arrangement to meet Willie completely slipped my mind. An hour or so went by before I was able to return to my hotel, where I was surprised and delighted to see Willie Jolley seated in the lobby, reading a book and armed with his ever-present smile. It took only a few minutes of talking with Willie for me to know that here was a young man destined for greatness.

Since that time, I have seen Willie Jolley continue to grow, to strive for greatness and to dream the big dream . . . and to pursue that dream. I've watched him grow from a well-received local speaker to one of the hottest young speaking talents in the country. When Willie told me about his book, I became excited. I know the level of enthusiasm that Willie invests in each project he undertakes, whether it is speaking, singing, hosting his radio show, or just shaking your hand. This book is Willie Jolley at his best.

It Only Takes a Minute to Change Your Life! is written the way Willie lives—with enthusiasm, excitement, and energy. The book is packed with inspirational and quickly digested ideas, anecdotes, and stories designed specifically for the person who's on the move and eager to get the most out of life. Read this book. Then reread it. Experience the love and care that Willie has taken with each anecdote and example. Meditate on the stories and jump into the success exercises. Grab hold of the goal-setting techniques—then let them grab hold of you. Dream the big dream, think the big thought, and dare to live life to the fullest.

Live your dream. Because you, like Willie Jolley, were destined for greatness! *It Only Takes a Minute to Change Your Life!* . . . enjoy the journey!

Introduction
by W Mitchell

The power of positive thinking is hardly a new idea. The concept of motivation hasn't just burst on the scene. But Willie Jolley packages both of these ideas in a brand-new way, injecting these power-packed motivational messages with his unflagging energy and enthusiasm. For years, Willie has offered his radio audience a bright spot in their day; a little caffeine for the spirit. His "Magnificent Motivational Minutes" have encouraged his listeners and inspired them to pursue their dreams and take control of their lives.

Many of us in the hectic, fast-paced field of public speaking have been using these minute motivators as a resource for years. In the very little time we have between planes and between speeches, we're able to get a lot of information, inspiration, and comfort from the messages that Willie Jolley has for us.

For as many years as Willie has been brightening the airwaves, his listeners have been begging him to share his insight with them in written form. This book, a compilation of Willie's Motivational Minutes, his personal reflections, and some terrific stories and ideas, is Willie's answer to those requests. Whether you dip into it a minute at a time or read it cover to cover in one sitting . . . you'll find yourself more inspired, more determined, and more thoughtful with every page. Even if you have only a minute, who knows, in that minute you might just change your life. The most important thing in any project is TO BEGIN. The old Chinese proverb says that the longest journey always begins with a single step. By making sure that you read the first page of this book, you will get to page 2. Read the first page, take the first step, and begin the journey, and by the time you finish just a few pages in this book you will be running and on your way . . . to reach your dreams. Do It Now! ALOHA!

Preface

"Great things can come in small packages." We have all heard this old adage, but I learned firsthand about the power of these words a few years ago, when I was making my living as a singer and jazz performer. While in graduate school I supported myself by singing with various performers across the country. I would perform on weekends and go to school during the week. One of the best experiences I had was as a background singer with the great jazz artist Jean Carne. When I first went out on the road with her, I found that she was not only a great singer but was also very unselfish about sharing the stage with the background performers. During a portion of the show she would always introduce the band members and singers and give them a chance to show what they could do. This would be our time to solo and showcase our talents. The problem was that due to the number of people in the band the musicians were asked to keep their solos to eight measures.

Surprisingly, they could not do it. They could not keep their solos to eight measures. They could not conceive that a great performance could be given in such a short time. Most of them would just start warming up at the eight-measure mark and the others would take so long that the bandleader would just have to cut them off because they took too much time, which was very embarrassing. I was the new kid on the block and definitely did not want to be embarrassed! I studied the other people and I made up my mind that I was going to create an entertaining and exciting eight-measure performance. I figured I needed to make it short and sweet, and get the maximum out of a minimum amount of time. So when it was my turn, I delivered a solo that had a beginning, a middle, and an ending. It involved the audience in a call and response, then a sing-song, where I sang a quick rap and rhyme, then closed with a big ending, all in eight measures. It was a big hit and immediately became a popular part of the show. From that experience I learned it doesn't take a long time to make a positive impression and to get your point across! It's not important how much time you have, the key is what you do with the time you've been given.

That experience also taught me that with limited time you must make the best of what you've got to work with. It taught me the importance and power of brevity. It taught me that great performances can be short and succinct. In fact, one of the greatest performances of all time was one of the shortest. It was a speech given by Abraham Lincoln at the Gettysburg battlefield, called the Gettysburg Address. It was a short speech, less than five minutes in length, yet it has been called one of the greatest speeches of all times. In fact, the principal speaker for that Gettysburg program, Edward Everett, said that he wished he had been as effective in two hours as Lincoln had been in five minutes.

It does not take a long time to make a point, give a message or in fact, to change a life—it only takes a minute! As I progressed through life I remembered that lesson. Later, I started singing jingles and performing for commercials. I had sixty seconds to tell a story and sell the product. Again, I used the same concept and learned to deliver my message in a short period of time. The ability to tell the story quickly kept me very busy as a jingle singer.

I didn't forget the concept when I started public speaking, and I decided to develop some programs that would appeal to an audience in a short period of time. I envisioned programs that were informational, motivational, inspirational, and entertaining yet short and compact. I wanted to give a lot in a little bit of time. Time is very precious, and people are always rushing. They need motivation and often they need it in a hurry. The result was "The Magnificent Motivational Minute" radio series—one-minute motivational messages that are entertaining, informational, inspirational, and motivational.

This book is written to share that concept with you. It contains stories and thoughts that are designed to be short and quick but leave a lasting impression, ideas that are designed to give the maximum in a minimum time. In an age of Minute rice, instant coffee, fast food, quick cash, and phone loans, we now are happy to present "minute motivation"! The Magnificent Motivational Minute Book: *It Only Takes a Minute to Change Your Life.*

As my friend James Carter, the success strategist, says, "This book is designed to help you to take the tip from the top, the drip from the drop, and be the cream of the crop!"

The Magnificent Minute!

For so many years I thought, as do most people, that a minute was an insignificant amount of time. I figured that the only significant use of a minute was just to make hours, which were more important. I would hear people say "I'll be there in a minute" or "Wait a minute" when they really didn't mean a minute. They were actually talking about ten, fifteen, twenty minutes, or longer. A minute was just a figure of speech, something that we all took for granted.

As I grew older I realized that great things can come in small packages. I realized that a minute was not only vital but that it was the starting point of all success. We must be mindful of the fact that, just as pennies create dollars, minutes create hours. The difference is that if you throw away your pennies you have the capability to make more, as many as you want. But your time is not the same. You have a limit on the time you have on this earth, a limit on the number of minutes that you have to live. You must therefore be mindful of time and respectful of the minutes that make the hours, that make the days, that make the months, that ultimately make the years. Once lost, that minute cannot be recaptured. What you do with your minutes will ultimately determine what you do with your life!

In fact, time is one of the few commodities on this earth

that is equally distributed, where no one person has an advantage over another. We all have twenty-four hours to each day, 1,440 minutes. No one is given an hour more or an hour less. Everyone has twenty-four hours and there is absolutely nothing anyone can do to add more time to the day. It does not matter how much money you have or how much influence you command. The richest of the rich and the poorest of the poor have the same amount of time. Donald Trump has no more time than my friend Bobby, who washes windows at the local gas station. Bobby is a very capable and articulate person who has had some hard times and some tough breaks and has never been able to see himself overcoming the circumstances. He has never been able to reach his full potential. These two men have the same amount of time afforded them, **but the key is what they do with the time they are given**.

If we think of time in relation to water, we can see that most of us do not really think much of a single drop of water. But when that single drop of water is connected with more single drops of water it can become a raging river, and when harnessed can be one of the most powerful forces on this earth. The same is true for minutes. Singularly they are not highly considered, but in each minute is the potential for greatness. And when these minutes are harnessed and wisely used, they, too, can generate great power. *It Only Takes a Minute to Change Your Life*!

One of the major reasons that pushed me to write this book was the response I received from the listeners of my daily radio program, "The Magnificent Motivational Minute." I was amazed at the number of people who contacted me by phone, fax, mail, or just stopped me on the street. These people were excited about the concept of short, quick motivational ideas, "minute motivations." They told their friends to listen and the station got more and more calls and letters about the show. I received numerous calls from listeners who wanted a copy of one script or another. The idea of putting together a book of the scripts crossed my mind, but it was just not a priority.

One day I received a letter from a young woman whose

life had been changed by the motivational minute, and her letter had a major impact on me. This young woman had recently graduated from college and was having no success in finding a job. She was looking and looking, getting no positive responses. She became more and more despondent. She got to the point where she was in a state of total depression, so down that she just didn't see a reason for getting out of bed in the morning. She would stay in bed and sleep all day, and soon gave up on her job search because she felt that there was no use in trying anymore. She felt the situation was hopeless.

One morning while lying in bed she stumbled upon a radio station broadcasting "The Magnificent Motivational Minute" program. She said that she heard something in that morning's Motivational Minute that created a spark inside her and made her see life a little differently. That particular Motivational Minute has become one of my trademark shows and is one of my most popular shows. It is called "The Lion and the Gazelle," and it changed this woman's life.

🕐 The Lion and the Gazelle

Today's step for success is that we must see every day as an opportunity that demands that we give our all, do our best. We must see success not only as a destination, but also as a journey that is constantly filled with adventure and challenges. If we are willing to meet those challenges, then we can live life to the fullest. Friends, every morning in Africa a gazelle wakes up and knows that it must run faster than the fastest lion or it will be killed and eaten. Also every morning in Africa a lion wakes up and knows it must outrun the slowest gazelle or it will starve to death. It doesn't matter whether you are a lion or a gazelle, when the sun comes up you'd better be running! Remember that all things are possible if you can just believe. This is Willie Jolley, have a Great Day!

She heard the show that morning and realized she had to make a decision. *She could either act on life or life would act on her*. Then she had to follow up the decision with action, *she had to do something*. She told me that a light went on inside her head and she had a new perspective. In that moment she suddenly believed that she could not only get a job but that she could get the job she wanted. The key was that she had to get up and get started in order to get something going in her life.

That young woman got up and got started on her goal, and started listening to the show every day. And every day she became stronger and stronger and more committed to making her dreams come true. Initially she had no success in her job search, but she did not give up because she now had a new determination, a new mind-set. She kept listening and kept looking and within a few weeks not only did she find a job but she found one in her field, one that paid her more than she had originally been seeking!

She wrote me a wonderful letter and asked if I would send her the written copies of the scripts so she could read them and share them with her friends and family. I realized at that moment it was imperative that I make the time to compile these scripts and share them with others, because people are desperately in need of motivation and encouragement. There is a great hunger for positive information, yet in the hectic pace of our day-to-day lives many people don't seem to have the time to pursue motivation and self-development. They need quick, short ways of getting motivated. They need instant motivation, motivation in a minute. So now I am happy to present motivation in a minute, **because it really only takes a minute, just a minute . . . to change your life!**

My goal is for this book to help you make the decision and take the initial action to change your life. My objective is that after you read this book you will have a new mind-set, a new determination, and it will motivate you to take action. If that occurs, then you will have started the process of changing your life, the transformation process from what you are to what you can be! I once heard that a mind once stretched by new ideas can never return to its original position. I hope that this book will stretch your mind to attain new ideas and get you to reach deeper within yourself to pursue your dreams. No matter how successful you are or how much you have achieved thus far, this book will motivate you to continue to push and thus to accomplish even more. Every minute is precious. Every minute is a gift, packed with power, and every minute has the potential to change your life . . . if you use it wisely.

⊕ Carpe Diem

Over the past few years we have heard more and more people talk about CARPE DIEM, SEIZE THE DAY! Robin Williams made it popular in his movie *Dead Poets Society*, and it has become popular on shirts and posters, "CARPE DIEM, CARPE DIEM . . . SEIZE THE DAY!" Yet, I say you must not only be aware of CARPE DIEM but you should also be aware of CARPE MOMENTUM, which means "SEIZE THE MOMENT"! We have found that some people are here one minute, and gone the next! Life is strange and so very unpredictable. I think about the story of the woman who loved dessert and decided to put off eating her favorite treat until later in the day—the problem was she was aboard the *Titanic*! Gordon and Brecher wrote a book called *Life Is Uncertain, Eat Dessert First*, which highlights this concept. Life is very uncertain and very unpredictable, therefore we should not only seize the day but we should also seize the moment . . . CARPE DIEM, and CARPE MOMENTUM!

It Only Takes A Minute To Change Your Life!

CHAPTER I

It Only
Takes a Minute
to Change Your Life!

It Only Takes A Minute (by Al Johnson)

Are you tired of crying and complaining
Tired of feeling like life don't treat you fair
Do you see so many others moving on
While you're steady going nowhere?

Have you maybe come to the conclusion
That there's nothing at all that you can do
Well just look in any mirror and you'll see
Who is really, truly stopping you!

It's up to every one of us
To take charge of our life and to make it what we want.
If you think that it takes too much time
Think again, cause I'm telling you it don't, the fact
  is . . .

It Only Takes, Only Takes a Minute
To make up your mind, that now is your time to make
  your run!
It Only Takes, Only Takes a Minute
Sixty seconds to begin, to decide to win, just get it on!

1

Start it off by checking your frustrations
Scream out loud that you've had it up to here
Get yourself so fired up to change
That you'll lose every doubt and fear

Then decide that you're really gonna do it
Cut yourself off from every other choice
What you say, make sure you really mean
You cannot just be making noise

Everybody's journey starts the same
With one single step, nothing more nothing less
Let the next step you take point the way
To you giving and you getting all the best, remember

It Only Takes, Only Takes a Minute
To make up your mind, that now is your time to make
*   your run!*
It Only Takes, Only Takes a Minute
Sixty seconds to begin, to decide to win, just get it on!

☽ The Importance of a Single Minute

Today we want to talk about the importance of a single minute, this minute you are investing in reading this page. It may not seem like a big deal, but let me tell you it is a major deal, because a minute is the starting point of building your dreams. From a great minute comes a great hour, and from a great hour comes a great day and from a great day comes a great week, then a great month, then a great year, and from there you can be the architect of a great lifetime and it starts with a single minute! That is why we must cherish every minute and use our minutes wisely. Dr. Benjamin Mays said it best: "I have only just a minute, only sixty seconds in it. Forced upon me, can't refuse it. Didn't seek it, didn't choose it, but it's up to me to use it. I must suffer if I lose it, give account if I abuse it. Just a tiny

2

little minute, but an eternity is in it." So ladies and gentlemen, use your minutes wisely!

Kipling wrote, "Fill the unforgiving minute with sixty seconds' worth of distance run." "Sixty seconds' worth of distance run" means to use your time wisely because the minute is very unforgiving. It does not care who you are or what your position is; it is unforgiving for you, for me, for the President, members of Congress, doctors, lawyers, and everyone else. Time waits for no one, so we must be mindful of our minutes and realize they are the most precious commodity that we possess. Once spent, they cannot be replaced!

Each person on this earth is given a limited measure of time to live. Also, each of us is given a daily measure of time, the hours of each day, which is absolutely the same for everybody. Rich people have no more time per day than poor people; short people have no more time than tall people; kings and queens have no more time than their subjects.

Each person is given twenty-four hours each day, 1,440 minutes that are credited to their account. When those minutes have been spent, you cannot buy any more minutes that day. When your day is over, when those 1,440 minutes have been used, you cannot purchase any more time, no matter how much money you have or how much power you possess.

🕐 Time Is Moving, Are You?

Friends, time waits for no one. It moves on and keeps moving on. It does not stop for anything or anybody. It doesn't matter how much money you have, how much power you have, or how much prestige you have—time keeps moving on; therefore, you have got to respect time and use it wisely, because time doesn't care who you are. Time is the great equalizer. From its standpoint everybody is equal. It gives the same divi-

dend to the rich as to the poor, to the powerful as to the weak, to the big as to the small. Everybody has the same amount of time, twenty-four hours per day, not one minute more. The key to success is not the time you have, because you've only got twenty-four hours, 1,440 minutes to each day—the key is what you do with the time you have! How do you use your time? Do you use it wisely, or do you squander your precious minutes? Do you fill your life with time a-wasting, or do you fill your time with life a-making? Your success or your failure depends on how you use your time. Time is moving on . . . are you?

Each minute is precious because it cannot be replaced. Once this day has been spent, we cannot change the time that has passed. Each day is its own separate unit of time and cannot be relived. Once gone, it is over and done with, so we must use it wisely, because we have no guarantee how much time we have on this earth. My friend Steve Hardiman sent me a wonderful quote that reads, "What I do today is important because I am paying a day of my life for it. What I accomplish must be worthwhile because the price is high!" Friends, it is critical that we use our minutes wisely because the price . . . is high!

🕐 There's No Time to Lose!

According to statistics the average lifespan in America is 79.5 years of age. If you are now 20, then according to current lifespan statistics, you have just over 700 months to live. If you are 30, then you have approximately 600 months to live. If you are 40, then you have approximately 480 months to live. If you are 50, then you have just over 320 months; if 60, then about 240 months; if 70, then approximately 120 months, and if you are 80 or above . . . then you are just blessed! Even though these are just numbers, we must be mindful that they have some relevance because none of us know how long we are going to live. We should not take our lives for granted. Even though lifespans are increasing we should realize that time is precious and we really have no time to lose. Live your life with gusto because there is no time to lose!

☽ Make Your Minutes Work for You!

We all have twenty-four hours per day, not a minute more or a minute less. The key to success is what you're doing with the minutes that you are given. Mike Murdock says that we all have twenty-four boxcars that we are given each day. Do you fill them with dirt or with diamonds? Bill Gates has twenty-four hours every day, so does my friend Bobby, the window washer. The difference is how they use the time they have. Bobby is a man who washes people's car windows at my local gas station in exchange for their spare change. He is very articulate and very personable, but he has resigned himself to being a window washer because he doesn't believe that he can do any better. Every time we talk he always says, "I'm gonna do it, I'm gonna do it, I'm gonna do more with my life!" But he never does. The next day he is back there washing windows for pennies when he has the potential to make dollars. He fills his minutes with dirt when he could fill them with diamonds. Bill Gates, on the other hand, also has twenty-four hours, but he uses his time differently. He fills his minutes with dollars rather than pennies. Life is difficult for us all, and offers unique challenges to each person. Some start off farther behind than others, but each of us can choose how we spend our time. Do we fill our hours with dirt or with diamonds? Do we fill our minutes with dimes or with dollars? No matter where we are in life, we do have a choice. Use your time wisely. Fill your time with diamonds and not dirt!

⏱ The Power of Decision!

How long does it take to change your life? Most people believe that it takes a long time, but that's a myth. In reality it only takes a minute! That's right, a minute! The minute you actually decide to change and decide to move in a different direction is the minute that you actually change your life. What takes a long time is getting ready to make a decision! You bounce around the ideas as to whether you should or you shouldn't, debating the issue of change. Many think about the idea for so long that they are caught up in the "Paralysis of Analysis." They debate it for so long that nothing actually gets done. But the minute you decide and take action is the minute you actually change your life. Dr. Howard Thurman, the great theologian, stated in one of his speeches, "The moment, the minute that this generation conquers fear, then that is the minute that the battle is won . . . the skirmishes will come, but the battle is won!" The moment, the minute we make the decision, and move on that decision, is the minute we change our lives!

My friends Jim and Naomi Rhode often start their seminars with the question "How do you achieve great things in life?" And as people mull around for the answer, Jim and Naomi answer the question. They say, *"You Just Decide To!"* The key to changing your life is first to make a decision. Og Mandino calls it "The secret of choice," Les Brown calls it "The dynamics of decision," Anthony Robbins says, "Your destiny is determined by your decisions." However you want to put it, the key is that you are where you are and what you are because of your choices, or lack thereof. Act on life or life will act on you! Either you decide or life will decide for you! How many of us have decided not to make a decision and life went on anyway and the decision was made for us? We all have! Yet we can take some control of our lives by making a decision and not waiting for life to decide for us. The minute you decide, and take action on that decision, is the minute you change your life! DECISION IS THE KEY TO CHANGING YOUR LIFE! Yet to make a decision you must first know where you want to go. You must first have a dream. **You've got to have a dream**!

CHAPTER II

To Do the Incredible, You Must Dream the Impossible!

As we look through the annals of time, we see that every great accomplishment, every outstanding achievement came about because someone was willing to go after that which was considered to be impossible! Whether it be inventors like Thomas Edison, Henry Ford, Alexander Graham Bell or the Wright brothers. Or whether it be social reformers like Martin Luther King, Jr., or Susan B. Anthony, who fought for women's right to vote, or Nelson Mandela, who did what others thought was impossible by going from a prisoner *in* South Africa to the president *of* South Africa. *To do the incredible, you must first dream the impossible!* After you dream the impossible then you must get motivated and make it happen!

What is motivation? Motivation is taken from the Latin word *motere* which means to take action. I personally like to think of motivation as having three specific parts, which I have stated for this book in a very simple way.

⏰ Conceive It, Believe It, and Achieve It!

Welcome to the Magnificent Motivational Minute, a minute that will inform, inspire, educate, and motivate;

a minute that can change your life. To fully understand the Motivational Minute, let's first define "motivation." Webster defines motivation as "something (as a need or desire) that drives or causes a person to act." I see motivation as having three parts: first is to get you to dream, to conceive of an idea, a concept; second, to get you to believe in your heart (the Bible says that all things are possible if you can just believe), the third part is to get you to decide to do something, to go after your dreams; to pursue your dreams and then to achieve your dreams. In short, to motivate you is to help you understand that if you can conceive it and believe it, then you can achieve it. If you can dream it, then you can do it. You can be great. Remember that all things are possible if you can just believe. Have a fantastic day!

All things truly are possible if you can dream big dreams. Believe in your dreams and then go after them with all that is within you. I remember when I decided to go out and follow my dream, to speak and motivate people. My co-workers told me I had to be crazy, as they stood at the door and watched me walk those 100 long steps to my old broken-down car. They laughed because they knew that the car was on its last legs and all I had to my name was $200. They said, "You must be insane! You're going to leave your good government job because you've got a dream? You want to do what?! You want to be a speaker? You want to start your own company? You want to write books? You want to do radio and television? You want to Be Great? *Stop Dreaming! Get Real!* You don't even have enough money to fix your car!" I could hear them laughing louder and louder with every step I took. The farther I walked, the louder they laughed! The last thing I heard them say was "He'll be back. He'll be back. Ha! Ha! Ha! He'll be back!"

Well, they were right! I did go back! But this time I returned as a consultant, driving a Mercedes-Benz . . . making about eight times as much as when I left! In just a few short years I had become the president of my own company and had a staff and a beautiful office. I had spoken to over one million people. I had written books and recorded albums and motivational books on tapes. I had a syndicated radio show and had just been elected president of the National Capitol Speakers Association. And I was having a ball!

Did the Mercedes, the staff, or the money make me a success? **NO!** Those were just the by-products of my learning the recipe for success. What was it? What was the key? What was the main ingredient? What was the thing that kept me from turning around and listening to my coworkers? What kept me from believing my coworkers and made me step out all by myself? What was the thing that was essential to my success? *What was it?* **It Was . . . the Power of a Dream and the Decision to Follow That Dream!**

⏱ You've Got to Have a Dream!

Every day is a brand-new day, a day unlike any other day, a brand-new opportunity to make your dreams come true. But in order for your dreams to become true, it is necessary for you to have a dream. You've got to have a dream, a goal—not just a resolution that you make on the first of January and forget by the fifteenth, but a goal, a target, a destination that you have made a commitment to. It is critical that you have a dream. Dr. Benjamin Mays said it so well when he said, "It must be borne in mind that the tragedy of life doesn't lie in not reaching your goal. The tragedy lies in not having a goal to reach for. It isn't a calamity to die with dreams unfulfilled, but it is a calamity not to dream. It is not a disaster to be unable to capture your ideal, but it is a disaster to have no ideal to capture. It is not a disgrace not to reach the stars, but it is a disgrace to have no stars to reach for. Not failure, but low aim, is sin!" Ladies and gentlemen, most people have

11

low aim or no aim and make little resolutions that they don't stick to. If you aim at nothing, that is probably what you will hit! Aim high, dream big dreams, set big goals, and, remember, all things are possible if you can just believe.

Have you ever wondered why some people can make a million dollars and lose it, make a second million and lose it, then make a third million, while others can hardly make ends meet? Why is it that some people no matter what they touch seems to turn to gold, while others can never quite hit the mark? The answer is that those people know the recipe for success. Just as there is a recipe for making a cake or pie, there is also a recipe for success. You all know someone who can make great cakes and pies, like my wife's Aunt Bubba. Aunt Bubba makes the best cakes, pies, and rolls I have ever tasted, and she makes them every day. Sometimes she has to double the quantity because people eat them up so quickly. But no matter how fast the pies and the rolls are eaten, she can make more. Why? Because Aunt Bubba knows the recipe!

Now, let's say someone comes to my aunt's house and loves the way the cakes and pies taste. So this person decides that they are going to go home and make some for themselves, but they do not have the recipe. So they go home and try, and fail, then they try again and fail, and try and fail and try and fail and, eventually, like most people, they give up. Well, that's what happens in life. Most people want to be successful, but they don't have the recipe. Most people go through life in a constant state of trial and error; they try and fail, then try and fail and try and fail, and eventually they give up. Statistics show that if you take one hundred people and start them at the same place, at the age of 19, by the time they are 65 only one will be wealthy, four will be financially secure, nineteen will still be working to simply survive, twenty-two will be deceased, and fifty-four will be flat broke and dependent on the government or their families for their survival. It doesn't have to be that way!

What is the common denominator of success? What do all successful people have in common? Ninety-nine percent of the time I get the same answer . . . MONEY! It is the number one answer whether I go to schools, colleges, trade associations, or corporations. It is the number one answer, but it is not the right answer. Money does not determine your success, but if you are successful you can have as much money as you need. Money is a result, a by-product of success, not the other way around. Case in point: Mother Teresa became a major success but she was not a rich woman. Yet if Mother Teresa were to go on television at noon on any day of the week and make a worldwide appeal for fifty million dollars, she would have if before the end of that day! Money does not determine success, but if you are successful you can have as much money as you need. Martin Luther King, Jr., was a major success, but he was not a rich man.

I had a teacher in junior high school who was always encouraging and inspiring me, no matter how much I misbehaved. Every day she would say to our class, "You're gonna be great, you're gonna be great!" That lady is not a rich woman, but she is a major success. Money in itself does not determine success, but if you're successful you can have as much money as you need.

What is the common denominator, the main ingredient for all success? It is the ability TO DREAM! To see things that are not yet a reality and see them as being a possibility. To be able to dream, to be able to develop a vision for your future. The Bible says in Proverbs 29:15, "Where there is no vision the people perish." Dreams are essential for success, no matter what else you may or may not have, one thing you must have is a dream. If you don't have a dream, how are you going to have a dream come true? Friends, you've got to have a dream!

⏱ Standing on the Verge; You Gotta Dream!

As I travel around the country speaking, there is one point I cannot stress enough: It is the importance of dreaming; the need to dream. In reviewing the lives of those who have made invaluable contributions to our society, one common element consistently comes up. They all understood the power of dreams. From Martin Luther King, Jr., to Walt Disney, to Thomas Edison, to Albert Einstein. The list goes on and on and on. Dreams are the seed for success. We're going to learn how to dream those dreams that change our lives. We'll learn how to dream, how to follow our dreams, and how to make them come true. If you can dare to dream, then you can dare to win. I'm excited because we are standing on the verge of a great adventure, and it's called living life to the fullest. Victor Hugo said, "An idea whose time has come cannot be denied!" Get ready, set, go! Let's start to dream! And let's start to live life to the fullest!

⏱ The Importance of Imagination

The importance of imagination was best impressed on me as a youth when I had the opportunity to meet Muhammad Ali. I was visiting my grandmother in Philadelphia and my mother was able to get tickets to see Muhammad Ali during the taping of a local television show. I was so excited I didn't know what to do. I couldn't wait until it was time to go to the television studio. We arrived and we even got front-row seats! The champ arrived and shook everybody's hand on the front row and I was so excited because I could now go home and tell all of my friends that I actually shook hands with Muhammad Ali!

I look back now and realize that shaking his hand was fine, but that would wash off. However, during the interview he said something that would not wash or wear

14

off. He planted a seed that grew, as I grew, and helped to shape my thinking. During the interview he was asked how he had revolutionized the boxing industry so that people flocked to see his fights. His reply was that he had imagination and that was the key to his success! He said, "You see I learned a long time ago that being good was simply not good enough, you've got to have imagination and you've got to dream."

Muhammad Ali developed a personality, a persona, that people either loved or they hated. Those who loved him came to see him win; those who hated him came to see him lose. Either way, every seat was taken! I learned something that day that will help me for a lifetime. I learned about the power of dreams. I learned that you've got to have imagination, that you've got to be creative, that you've got to have a dream!

⏱ The Dream Seed

Just as everything in life that grows is the result of a seed, the same is true for your dreams. Dreams are the starting point for success, the seed for success. If you take a corn seed, plant it and water it daily, it will grow into a cornstalk. If you take an acorn, plant it and water it daily, it will grow into an oak tree. The same is true for your dreams. If you can conceive the dream in your mind, plant it in your heart, and water it daily, then it, too, will grow. How do you water it? You water it by saying daily, "I believe I can, I believe I can, in fact I know can." Plant your dream deep, water it daily, and don't let the weeds of doubt choke it, and your dream can and will become a reality.

⏱ The Dreamer, Michael Jordan

One of my favorite examples of a dreamer is Michael Jordan. I heard a story about Michael Jordan that began by asking, "What made him such a great basketball player?" The answer was that when he was in the ninth grade Michael got cut from the basketball team for not being good enough. He went home and started to dream, because he wanted to prove to the coach that he had made a mistake. Once Michael could dream and see it in his mind, then he realized that he could do it. And once he realized he could do it, he went out on the court and did it. He dreamed it and he went on to become one of the greatest basketball players of all time. He understood that in life to be great you must be willing to dream and then to pursue your dreams and never let others keep you from reaching your potential. You, too, can fly high and reach the sky!

⏱ Hank Aaron, Dreaming in Slow Motion!

In an interview with Hank Aaron, author Robert Griessman stated that Hank Aaron was not just an exceptional athlete, but also used other tools to help him to become the top home-run hitter of all times. He used his ability to dream in combination with his exceptional ability to focus and concentrate. Mr. Griessman says that Hank Aaron would study pitchers throughout the league and concentrate on their strengths and weaknesses. He would then focus on what it would take for him to hit home runs off of them. Last, but not least, he would dream about the game and envision himself seeing the ball and focusing on it until he could control the speed of the ball in his thoughts, and then he could make it slow down right as it approached the plate. He would then hit the ball with all of his power and the result would be . . . a home run! He would combine the ability to dream with extreme focus; he would see home runs as a possibility, then he would make them into realities.

While I was speaking to a group of college students, one young woman told me that she was confused because she had dreams every night, and she hadn't seen any major difference in her life. She wasn't a success yet. I explained that there are different of kinds of dreams. One is the kind that you have at night where you just see pictures and stories in your mind. There are the good ones where everything is wonderful, and then there are the bad ones, which we commonly call nightmares. Some laughed and said they liked nightmares because they got to see a free scary movie without having to leave home, leave their beds, or even get up and turn on the television.

Another kind of dream is the daydream, where you drift off into faraway thoughts while you are still awake. Most times this happens in school or while you are at work, when you are supposed to be paying attention to someone or something else. The problem with daydreaming is that it is hard to learn or accomplish much when your body is in one place and your mind is in another. The last kind of dream is the one that makes the difference between success and failure: the dream to imagine.

⏱ The Dream to Imagine!

The type of dream that we want to concentrate on today is the kind of dream that was exhibited by Dr. Martin Luther King, Jr.: the Dream to Imagine. To see things as a possibility that are not yet a reality. We are capable of unbelievable things if we allow our minds to soar, if we can cut away the binds that limit us. If you stop and look around you right now, everything you see started in someone's imagination. The radio you listen to, the clothes you wear, the telephone you speak into, your home, your car, your office. These things didn't exist thousands of years ago, but thanks to someone's imagination they exist today. You, too, can use your imagination to do great things. Try it . . . you'll love it!

One of the questions I regularly get is, "Why dream?" Good question, WHY DREAM? There was a study in which college students were hooked up to machines that monitored their sleep patterns and brain waves to determine when they were dreaming. Dreams happen during REM (rapid eye movement) sleep. Every time the students started REM sleep patterns and the monitors registered that they were starting to dream, they were awakened. They had a reasonable amount of sleep but were not allowed to dream. After the first night, the students woke up feeling irritable; after the second night, they woke up edgy; after the third night, they woke up irrational; and, after the fourth night, they woke up psychotic and the experiment was stopped! The experiment proved that it is critical to dream while you are asleep because it helps to keep you stable. But it is also critical to dream while you are awake because dreams are the seed for success.

① Where Do Dreams Come From?

Dreams, where do they come from? Robert Schuller, noted minister and author, says that dreams do not come out of the blue but rather come out of the mind of God. God matches the dream with the dreamer, someone who will receive it, respect it, embrace it, claim it, live for it, and be willing to die for it. God gives to humans one of his greatest gifts, a dream. Yet it is up to us to receive it and let it grow, or to reject it and kill it. Proverbs 29:18 says, "Where There Is No Vision the People Perish." I believe in "Where There Is a Vision the People *Flourish*." We must dare to dream and dare to win!

I was speaking at Hampton University when one freshman asked a profound question: "How do you dream, when you cannot see a way out and you just can't see much hope?"

I have found that many people have given up on their dreams; they don't even remember how to dream and therefore don't think that they have a dream.

While in Los Angeles for a speech I had the occasion to go to dinner with a friend named John Alston. John is a magnificent speaker and is considered one of the top experts in education in America. He took me to a restaurant that featured live music, since he knew of my background in the music industry. As we waited for a table, we could hear some of the music and it was terrific. At the band's break we went up to the pianist and told him how much we enjoyed the music and how terrific we both thought he was. Then John asked him, "Friend, what is your dream?" The musician looked up and said, "I don't have a dream anymore, I gave up on it a long time ago." John and I looked at each other and then looked at the musician and said, "OH, NO! You cannot give up on your dream. No matter what you do, you cannot give up on your dream because to go on without a dream isn't really living, it is merely existing." We proceeded to talk to him until our table was ready, and then continued after the meal. He left that night a new man because he was ready to recapture his dream.

⏰ Hold Fast To Your Dreams

When I was in high school I remember one of my teachers discussing a Langston Hughes poem about dreams that stuck with me through the years. He told us to hold on to our dreams and that if our dreams die, then life is like a broken-winged bird. Friends, a broken-winged bird cannot fly! Too many people have given up on their dreams, and by giving up on their dreams they have in essence given up on their possibilities. Many people have been frustrated and discouraged by the challenges of life that we all must face in one form or another. Far too often we see them give up without even a fight, not realizing that dreams are the seed for success. Fight for your dreams, because the rewards can be "Oh, so sweet!"

🕐 If You Can Dream It . . .

Walt Disney said, "If you can dream it, you can do it." He didn't just say it because it was a nice-sounding phrase. He said it because he knew from personal experience that it was true. Walt Disney started as a simple cartoonist and went on to become one of the most successful entrepreneurs of all time. His story begins with his dropping out of school to join the army and then coming home and starting to draw cartoons, then getting a partner and going into the cartoon business, then having the business fail. Walt was broke then and he had to get handouts to survive. He decided to go out to California and start over, but he didn't have any money, and so he sold everything he had to get enough money to get a one-way ticket to California. He went with forty dollars, an imitation-leather suitcase, one mismatched suit, and some drawing materials. But he also had a dream. He got to California and started a new company. He had setbacks and endured two nervous breakdowns, but he still had a dream. He eventually had to sell his car and mortgage his home to start Disneyland, but he still had a dream. He borrowed to the hilt and was turned down by lots and lots of people, but he still had a dream. Many laughed at him and called him crazy, but he never let go of his dream. Disneyland opened and became the biggest attraction in America and he became a multimillionaire. If you can dream it, you can do it!

🕐 Gotta Dream

I have found that a dream mixed with confidence, determination, persistence, and massive belief will grow into a reality. The bigger the dream, the bigger the rewards. Martin Luther King, Jr., had a dream. He was confident, determined, and persistent, and he became great. Mary McLeod Bethune had a dream. She wanted to start a college for black students who normally would not be able to attend college. She started the school in Daytona Beach, Florida, with six dollars to her name, but she was in possession of something more powerful: A DREAM. Today Bethune Cookman College is one of the great schools of higher education in this country and Mary McLeod Bethune is remembered as one of America's greatest women because she believed in her dream and had confidence, determination, and persistence. Spud Webb is five feet six inches tall. He wanted to play basketball, but everyone said he was too short, that it could never happen. But Spud Webb had a dream, a big dream. A few years ago Spud Webb won the dunk contest for the National Basketball Association. Jose Feliciano was born in Puerto Rico, he was born blind, in a time when blind people were told that they were not able to do anything but to get a silver cup and beg for money. But Jose refused to accept that idea because he had a dream, a big dream. Jose found an old piece of guitar and taught himself how to play. He practiced day and night and night and day, sometimes until his fingers bled. Today Jose Feliciano is one of the greatest musicians of our time. He wrote a song we sing every Christmas called "Feliz Navidad." He is a multimillionaire. You've got to have a dream. What is your dream? Whatever it is, you can achieve it . . . if you believe it, and have confidence, determination, and persistence. As Dexter Yager, the former truck driver who built a multimillion-dollar business, wrote, "If the Dream Is Big Enough, the Facts Don't Matter!"

⊙ The Mind Is a Marvel, Use It!

Psychologists and doctors for years have been saying that we only use a small percentage of our mental capacity. Some say we only use about 15 percent of what the mind is capable of. The mind is like a movie camera and can replay things that have happened in the past, which is our memory. But it can also "pre-play" things that are going to happen in the future, which are our dreams. We all know how to replay our past, but very few know how to pre-play the future and how to make those dreams come true. If we can learn to dream and then dare to go after those dreams, we can do great things. Use all of your mind.

Once you've got a dream, is that all there is to it? NO! It is not enough just to have a dream, you must follow the dream and make it a reality. The dream is just the beginning. To make it a reality you have got to accept it, believe it, and then go after it and achieve it.

Once you conceive of your dream and you believe it and nourish it, then that dream will start to grow. Then you've got to be concerned about the weeds that will crop up all around your dream and start to kill it, strangle it, choke it! I like to call those weeds the *DreamBusters*. The *DreamBusters* are very similar to ghostbusters. A ghostbuster's job is to kill, destroy, eliminate, or get rid of the ghost. The *DreamBuster*'s job is to kill, destroy, eliminate, or get rid of your dreams.

The difference is that ghostbusters are highly identifiable: they stand out in a crowd. They have proton packs, zippers, funny cars, and funny clothes. You can tell a ghostbuster a mile away. *DreamBusters* do not stand out in a crowd. They have no funny clothes and have no identifiable characteristics. In fact, they may look a whole lot like your best friend, classmate, coworker, cousin, or someone in your own household.

Once you find a *DreamBuster*, you have two options: one is to change them into dream-makers; inspire, encourage and enlighten them to the possibilities that exist. If this does not work, then you've only got one other option: LEAVE THEM ALONE! Get as far away from them as north is to south and east is to west. Get away and stay away, because if you don't they will bust your dreams and take you down with them.

There are many types of *DreamBusters*, but there are five major *DreamBusters* that are common and active in killing dreams today. The #1 *DreamBuster* is . . . "**Us**." That's right . . . "**Us**." We are our own worst enemies. Most often we talk ourselves out of our own best ideas!

⏰ The Rabbi's Son

There is a parable about the rabbi's son who goes to live in a neighboring town. When the son returns home the father asks him if the town was different. The son says, "Yes, Father, they teach you to love your enemy." The father protested, "Well, we teach the same thing here." The son replied, "Yes, but they teach you to love the enemy within!" Most people go through life searching for the enemy. They look high and they look low. They look here and they look there, they look up and they look down, they look everywhere! They look everywhere for the enemy. Never realizing, as T. D. Jakes says, "That the enemy . . . is within-a-me!" Pogo said it so aptly, "We have found the enemy and he is us!"

⏰ The Enemy on the Inside

You may ask why I spend so much time talking about dreams. The reason is because dreams are essential to success. Yet, many people reject their dreams and are in reality their own worst enemies. How many of us have been given a thought, a dream, or a vision and we've talked ourselves out of it by saying, "I can't do that! I just can't do that!" You can do anything you want to do. An old African proverb says, "If you can overcome the enemy on the inside, the enemy on the outside won't be able to do you any harm. God would not give you a dream that you could not achieve. If you can dream it, then you can do it. If you are willing to accept it, conceive and believe it . . . then you can achieve it!

⏱ It is Not The Mountain . . . It Is Ourselves!

How many of us have had at least one good idea in our lifetime? All of us have! Now, how many of us have talked us out of at least one good idea? We all have! Not realizing that one good idea could be all that it takes to change your life. Yet we have all talked ourselves out of good ideas that could have changed our lives. In an interview Sir Edmund Hillary was asked what was the biggest challenge he faced in becoming the first man to reach the top of Mt. Everest. The biggest obstacle, he said, was to overcome the psychological barrier and to keep from talking himself out of trying. The major obstacle was to give up without trying. Often we never accomplish the goal because we simply never try! We talk ourselves out of trying by "saying it's impossible, it can't be done." Most times we do not . . . because we try not. Yet, once Sir Edmund Hillary got to the top of Mt. Everest and showed that it could be done, it immediately became easier for others. People saw that it was possible and then said, "Maybe I can too!" Now there are even tours to the top of Mt. Everest. As Sir Edmund Hillary so brilliantly stated, "It was not the mountain we conquered, it was ourselves." Do it now! Conquer your mountain today!

Each time you achieve something, even small things, you are adding to your self-esteem, your self-image, your self-concept. You are making small deposits into your own bank

24

of confidence. You are subconsciously saying, "I'm all right, I'm okay. Look what I did! If I can do that then I can achieve more." It starts with little accomplishments that lead to big accomplishments. But it starts with you, believing in yourself and conquering the enemies on the inside!

The #2 *DreamBuster* is to hang out with small-minded, itty-bitty, negative-thinking people! Particularly those who like to use the word "can't." You know, the people who say, "You can't do this you're too old." "You can't do that you're too young." "You can't do this you don't have enough education." "You can't do that you don't have the right qualifications!" "You can't do that, it will never work! You might as well give up and save yourself the time and aggravation." "You can't do this, you can't do that, you can't, you can't, you can't." STOP THE MADNESS! You can do anything you really want to do. If you can dream it, then you can do it—if you are willing to fight for it!

Alan Torgeson sent me this poem that states this so well:

Some of the most dangerous people are not the ones
Who hit you with clubs, or rob you with guns
They won't be the enemies who attack your character
    traits
Or try to belittle your abilities right in your face
No, the most dangerous people are small-minded friends
Whose negative talk crush your self-image and your
    desire to win
They do not threaten your life at the point of a gun
Rather they steal your dreams by saying that it just
    cannot be done
When pointing to others doing what you dream you can
    do
They say, "You can't do it, it won't happen for you"
It does not matter that their words are untrue
You listen anyway, thinking they know you better than
    you

*So you are robbed of your dreams and your hopes to
     succeed*
Robbed of the blessing that you could have received
Robbed of your faith that says that "You Can"
Robbed by an ignorant, small-minded friend
So the most dangerous ones
Are not the ones with the clubs or the guns
But the ones who keep telling you that it cannot be done
*For that which is stolen by a burglar can be gotten
     again*
But who can replace your dream and your desire to win!

⏰ The Sun Always Shines, But . . .

The sun always shines, but some days the clouds cover
up the sunshine! No matter how positive you are, it is
important to associate with those who are positive and
encourage you rather than those who are negative and
discourage you. There are two types of people in life:
Those who add to you and those who subtract from you,
those who deposit and those who withdraw. You must
decide which ones you want around you. It's like a bank
account: People will either deposit and add to your
dreams or they will subtract and take from your
dreams. If the negative naysayers continue to take and
withdraw from your dream, eventually your dreams will
come up "insufficient funds." The next step is bank-
ruptcy, giving up on your dreams. Then you start to
settle for what life throws at you instead of determining
your own destiny. Folks, this is not a dress rehearsal;
this is it. Follow your dreams and hang with those who
add to your account.

⏰ Look for the Good!

Do you know people who are always negative? Always
looking for, and finding, the bad in life? People who are

always whining and complaining about how bad things are. Nothing is ever right. Either it's too hot or too cold; too sweet or too sour; too hard or too soft. Too this or too that. Nothing is ever right! We must help those people to look for and find the good in life. Even a broken clock is right twice a day!

If we really care for those negative people then we must help them to realize that behind every cloud is a silver lining, if you are just willing to look for it. Share with them that positive people not only enjoy life more, but statistics show that they live longer! Help your friends to see the positive or they will help you to see more of the negative. Continue to look for the good in life, and most times you will find it!

⊙ Hammer . . . Why Not?

I had the opportunity to meet the rap artist Hammer. During our conversation I inquired if it was true what I had read about him in *Reader's Digest*. He said it was true, very true. Ten years ago Mr. Hammer was dancing and rapping outside the Oakland baseball stadium. He sold his homemade tapes to people going into the stadium to see the Oakland A's play. Many would put contributions into a cardboard box, as he exhibited his dancing and rapping talents on the street outside the stadium. His friends would come by and laugh at him and say, "Man, you can't dance. You can't rap! Why don't you stop all this foolishness? It's embarrassing." He told them he believed he could rap and could dance and that he had a dream. "A dream?" They laughed in his face. Well, Mr. Stanley Kirk Burrell, otherwise known as Hammer, went on to be listed in *Forbes* magazine as one of the wealthiest entertainers in the world. Many of those same friends who used to laugh at him eventually became employees of his. Do not, I repeat, do not listen to, hang out with, associate with people who like to use the word "can't." They will kill your dreams.

⏰ The Man In The Mirror

"You can't do that." "You just don't have what it takes." "You're not good enough." These statements are common tools of *DreamBusters*. They are frequently associated with people who talk us out of our best ideas and biggest dreams. The problem is that the main person who makes these statements is the person we see every day in the mirror. It is us! Many of us are our own worst enemies. We talk ourselves out of our best dreams and ideas by telling ourselves "We can't do it." "We don't have what it takes." "We are not good enough!" We all have experienced times when we doubt ourselves, and we doubt our abilities and therefore squelch what could be very profitable and productive activities, simply because we don't think we can! Well, I've said it before and I'll keep saying it: If you can control the enemy on the inside, the enemy on the outside cannot do you any harm. In reaching our potential, we must always start with self. First we must work on our own self-image. We must develop an "I can and I will" attitude and eliminate all negative self-talk as soon as it starts to enter our minds. Talk to yourself and tell yourself, "I can, oh yes I can." Greet yourself in the mirror every day and say, "You are one of the greatest people that the world has ever known and you are going to do unbelievable things today." Start with the person in the mirror, and then you can start to change those outside the mirror!

⏰ Your Words Speak Volumes

Most people do not have to wait for someone else to talk them out of their dreams, they will do it themselves! They use words that limit their vision and keep them from even giving their dreams a fighting chance. You must stop using negative words and start using positive, affirming words. This poem is one my daughter shared with me. The author is unknown but the message is very clear.

> *Did Is a Word of Achievement*
> *Won't Is a Word of Retreat*
> *Might Is Word of*
>   *Bereavement*
> *Can't Is a Word of Defeat*
> *Ought Is a Word of Duty*
> *Try Is a Word of the Hour*
> *Will Is a Word of Beauty*
> *Can Is a Word of Power*
>   AUTHOR UNKNOWN

Your words speak volumes. Use words that inspire you, not words that deflate you!

Can't is a Word That Must Be Ignored

Can't is a word that must be ignored
In the quest to conquer your dreams
This is a secret that others have learned
Who have done incredible things
They learned to conceive it and then to believe it
And found that their dreams could come true
If they were willing to fight for it,
With all of their might, for it!
Doggedly drive for it,
Struggle and strive for it,
If they were willing to give
Their all in the quest
Learn to believe and learn to say yes
If they learn to say yes to their hopes and their
    dreams
If they learn to say yes to all the incredible things
Then life would respond with unlimited zest

And they would've learned to excel in life's impossible tests!

WILLIE JOLLEY

We must make a determined decision that we will not associate with negative, small-minded people who bust your dreams and rob you of your confidence. Unfortunately, sometimes it is the people who are in our inner circle and who really love us. They are not trying to be mean-spirited or discouraging, but they just have "Possibility Blindness." They figure it will be too difficult and too painful if we do not reach these big dreams. Well, let me let you in on a secret, "IT'S PAINFUL EITHER WAY!" If you do nothing, it is painful! Yet if you go out to conquer the world, it, too, is painful. So my theory is if you must go through pain anyway . . . YOU MIGHT AS WELL GO FOR THE GUSTO!

I know about the effect that one negative person can have on your psyche and your self-image. In the ninth grade I used to play trumpet in a band and we would play at little dances on weekends. One day my parents said to me, "Why aren't you singing with that band? You sing around the house and you sing at church and at school. You're a good singer. You should be singing with that band." That evening I went to band practice and asked the guys if I could sing that night. Everyone said okay, so I started to sing. All the guys said it sounded okay, except one, who was the lead singer, who I thought was one of my best friends. "Willie, you can't sing! You sound terrible!" he said. Then he started laughing and the mob mentality took over and everyone else started laughing. I was so humiliated and embarrassed that I wanted to cry. But I couldn't let my buddies see me cry, so I acted like I agreed. I picked up my trumpet and went over to the corner and vowed to myself that I would never sing again as long as I lived! For three years I kept that vow. I didn't sing at home; I didn't sing at school; I wouldn't even sing at people's birthday parties when everyone sang "Happy Birthday" because I was ashamed. They had planted the seed in me that I couldn't sing, but I had made it grow, from a little seedling to a redwood tree. I actually believed that I couldn't sing!

One night, while I was playing my trumpet in a night-club, the band leader got a note saying the singer was sick and couldn't make it. He looked around and his eyes landed on me and he said, "Willie, you've got a nice speaking voice, come on over and sing for us!" I told him, "No, I can't sing!" He responded, "Come on over and sing!" I then replied, "No! I'm not gonna sing for you or anyone else!" Then he became angry and said, "I want you to sing!" And we began to argue back and forth until he finally said, "You either sing or you're *fired*!" At that point it became an easy choice! I needed that job!

But before I started singing I closed my eyes and visualized how I wanted it to turn out. Then I started singing with all that was within me. I sang as loud as I could and as strong as I could! When I opened my eyes people in the audience had stopped dancing and were just looking and clapping. Then I sang more and they clapped more! I sang and they clapped and I sang and they clapped. Finally at the end of the night people were lined up to my right and to my left and all around me asking could I sing at their weddings, at their graduations, at their churches, at this event, at that event. It finally hit me, my friend had lied to me!

Well, since that time I have sung at Carnegie Hall, at Lincoln Center in New York, at the Kennedy Center and Constitution Hall in Washington, D.C. I have sung on records, tapes, on jingles on radio and television. I have been around the country singing because I stopped listening to the *DreamBuster*. Stop listening to negative people who like to use the word "can't." They will kill your dreams!

⏱ The Richest Place In The World!

If I were to ask you, "Where is the richest place in the world?" I am sure that some would say the mint in Washington, D.C. Others would say Fort Knox, and

others would say the gold and diamond mines that populate the African continent. But all would be wrong. The richest place in the world is the graveyard! That's right, the graveyard. In it lie all the people who had great ideas that would have made them wealthy, but they listened instead to some negative person who used the word "can't" and they believed them. Then they took those great ideas with them to their graves! Their best song . . . unsung! Their best invention . . . undone! Their best book . . . unwritten! Their best speech . . . ungiven! Why? Because they listened to some negative person who used the word "can't." Do not, I repeat, do not take your riches with you to your grave!

Remember that *DreamBusters* can be changed! You must encourage them, enlighten them, and help them to grow. You have to prove to them that it is not only possible but very do-able.

But there are times when you have to just ignore them and make a commitment to yourself that you will not hang around them until they grow in consciousness. If not, they will carry you down with them. Do not, I repeat, do not let them bust your dreams and bring you down. If you cannot bring them up to your level, THEN LEAVE THEM ALONE! Do not let them bring you down to theirs!

Many times they will see from your example that it is possible. And if it is possible for you, then maybe they will start to believe that it is also possible for them. In life sometimes all you need is a MAYBE! Just a Maybe!

⏱ Maybe, Just Maybe!

Can you lift a car? No? Would you try? No? Why? Because your mind tells you that it is impossible to lift a car, so you will not even attempt to do something that your mind says is impossible. Yet there have been numerous accounts of people who have lifted cars in adverse situations. There are countless stories of parents whose children or loved ones were trapped in cars due to accidents and they defy logic to lift the car. They do the impossible! Why? In those situations they move beyond the thought of impossible. You, too, can move beyond thoughts of impossible, if you can just learn to think "MAYBE!" There are four levels of thoughts which determine our ability to achieve. First, there is the level of utter impossibility, where we won't even consider trying. Next is the level of doubt, where at least 51 percent of our being says that we don't think we can do it and so we tend not to try. Then there is the level of hope, where at least 51 percent says, "I think I can! Maybe!" Once you get a "maybe," you are much more apt to try. Finally, there is the level of certainty, where the mind says, "We can definitely achieve the goal." Once you try, your chances of achieving the goal rises tremendously. In life sometimes all you need is a maybe, just a maybe, because if you have a maybe you will at least try. If you try, then you have a chance of succeeding. But if you don't try, then you are guaranteed not to achieve it. You will always miss 100 percent of the shots you don't take! Give your best shot, think maybe!

The third *DreamBuster* is FEAR—fear that keeps you from even trying, fear that shackles and strangles your initiative to try. Studies show that there are only two innate fears, only two fears that babies come to this earth with, the fear of falling and the fear of loud noises. All other fears are learned behaviors. Franklin Roosevelt said, "There is nothing to fear but fear itself"; while Eleanor Roosevelt said, "If you identify the fear, look at it and then go toward it . . . then it will disappear!" Action is the cure for fear!

🕐 Fear Not

Today I want to share a quote with you from the book *Success Is Never Ending and Failure Is Never Final* by Dr. Robert Schuller. "Fear not that you might make a mistake believing in your dream. Fear rather that if you don't go for it you might stand before God and he'll tell you that you could have succeeded if you had just had more faith.

Fear not that you might fail. Fear rather that you will never succeed, if you never try and are unwilling to take risks. Fear not that you might be hurt. Fear rather that you might never grow if you wait for painless success."

Friends, fear not, but rather dare to dream. The old man said to the young man when comforting him on his fears, "Why not go out on a limb? Isn't that where the fruit is? It is impossible to reach second base if you are afraid to leave first base. You've got to have a dream and then dare to act on that dream and you can achieve great things. Fear not, my friends, fear not!

We all have fears, we were born with them as a protection mechanism in order that we use care in making decisions and avoid danger, but fears were not meant to shackle and hinder us from achieving our greatness. We have a choice to either have faith in our fears or faith in ourselves and our possibilities. As a friend shared with me:

Fear sees obstacles, Faith sees opportunities
Fear sees problems, Faith sees possibilities
Fear sees stumbling blocks, Faith sees stepping-stones!

It is your choice, you can either have faith in your fears or in ourselves. Have Faith in You! David Schwarz wrote in *The Magic of Thinking Big* that the cure for fear is action. Identify your fears and then move towards them. Take

action and they will disappear. Have faith, take action and
FEAR WILL DISAPPEAR!

⏱ Don't Worry, Be Happy!

**Don't worry! Be happy! Choose to be happy, because
you ultimately make the choice. You can either choose
to worry about life and what will happen in the future,
or you can choose to be happy, to enjoy life and to live
life to the fullest. It is a choice. The word *worry* comes
from the word "to choke," to strangle, and it is an
extension of fear. Fear is crippling, it shackles those
who could do great things and keeps them from even
attempting that which they could possibly achieve. Fear
chokes and kills dreams and creativity and the most
interesting thing about fear is that it is a learned be-
havior. Psychologists state that there are only two fears
that we are born with: the fear of falling and the fear
of loud sounds. All other fears are learned. They are
usually a misuse of the imagination. The imagination
was created for us to dream and see positive things that
are not yet a reality, and see them as being a possibility.**

**Many times in life we use our minds to think of every
possible problem that could arise. Our minds are created not to think up problems but rather to think up
solutions. After thinking up the solutions, then our
minds are to be used to think about how to make the
dreams into realities. Don't let fear choke you. Release
your fear, bust it, break it, forsake it, leave it, and let
it go. Look fear in the eye, challenge it, and it will go
away. Fear cannot stand action. Go after your dreams.
Don't worry; be happy! Or should I say, Be Jolley!**

⏱ Faith and Courage vs. Fear and Doubt

Michael Kelly is a tremendous speaker and trainer from Virgina Beach, VA, whom I like to call "the Professor" because of the outstanding ideas and information that he shares with his motivation. In his programs, Michael tells a powerful story about Faith and Courage vs. Fear and Doubt that he allowed me to share with you.

Once upon a time the two evil brothers, Fear and Doubt, were going around from house to house knocking on people's doors. When the people would answer the door, Fear and Doubt would rush in and ransack their houses and turn their lives upside down, leaving them too afraid to live their dreams. Fear and Doubt continued to go from house to house, from city to city and from state to state, destroying people's hopes and dreams. Then one day Fear and Doubt came to a new place and saw a beautiful big house and said "Let's go there! We can really do some damage." Fear and Doubt ran up to the door and knocked, but they did not know this was the home of their mortal enemies, Faith and Courage. Fear and Doubt knocked harder and harder and grew angrier and angrier. Finally Faith and Courage opened the door. And when they opened the door . . . there was no one there! They looked up the street, and looked down the street and they saw no one. Because, in the face of Faith and Courage . . . Fear and Doubt always DISAPPEAR!!!

The last major *DreamBuster* is Settling for Mediocrity, when excellence is just a few steps away. This *Dream-Buster* is commonly seen in our young people who believe the lie that being smart is being a nerd! It is manifested in our adults who settle for mediocrity on their jobs and rationalize it by saying, "It's close enough!" They settle for close enough when excellence can be achieved with just a little bit more effort.

🕐 Excellence Makes the Difference

In America we live in a pyramidal society, where there are lots of people at the bottom of the pyramid and a few people at the top. The people at the bottom are barely making ends meet from day to day, simply living from hand to mouth. The people at the top are those who are prospering and thriving. In every community and every geographic area, there are lots of people at the bottom and fewer people at the top. Many of the people at the top started at the bottom but rose to the top. Why? Because they refused to settle for mediocrity. They pursued excellence and began to rise. It's the Crème de la Crème Principle. The cream will rise to the top. I saw Oprah Winfrey on one of the nightly interview shows and she was asked how, from a broken home and from being a troubled teen, she had risen to her status as one of the most powerful women in television. Her answer was that she made a commitment to pursue excellence in everything she did. Initially, she did not look like a television or movie star. She was not svelte or thin or overly glamorous, but she pursued excellence with a passion. And excellence is like truth. You can push excellence down, try to cover it up, or try to ignore it. But no matter what you do to it, it always rises to the top. We must always pursue excellence in all that we do. Strive for excellence and your dreams will start to rise to the top!

My assistant Barbara pursues excellence with everything that she does. I asked her her secret for making the commitment to excellence, and she shared a verse that she keeps on her desk: "Success comes to those who build their house with unremitting purpose, stone by stone. Taking as great care with the last, as they do with the first, and always staying mindful that the most important stone is the one that they lay at that moment!'' Excellence always pays the best dividends!

⏲ Excellence Is the Best Job Security

As you and I both know, today there is no such thing as job security. People are losing their jobs at record rates. They are faced with the new trend called downsizing, or rightsizing, and all the other sizings. Whatever you call it, people are losing jobs faster than any time in previous history. Even though you cannot control what decisions a company will make, you can control your employment status. How? By making excellence your call letters and by developing a mind-set that makes you the CEO of Y.O.U. I like to share the story about a friend whose company went under but she had developed a reputation for excellence. Within a week of her being let go, a former coworker searched for her and hired her for another better paying job. Why? Because the former coworker remembered her desire for excellence. If the Chicago Bulls were sold, do you think Michael Jordan or Scotty Pippen would have a hard time getting a new job? I don't think so! Excellence is always the best job security. You might not be able to control what happens to your present job but you can control your employability. Remember, no matter where you are or what you do, somebody is always watching you and remembers what you do! Be excellent and take control of your future!

The next step to success is to decide to add the "do" to the dream. Take action on your dreams! The decision to act is a critical part of the process because action is absolutely necessary to make dreams come true.

⏰ A Dream, Then a Do!

We've been talking about dreams and goals and how they are the seed for success. They are the starting point for success. But once you have your dreams, you need to learn how to actualize them, how to make them into realities. Well, after you dream, you must decide to "do." You need to do something about your dreams. You have to pursue your dreams. You must "go for it" and not "for-go it"! For faith without works is really no faith at all. First you need a dream, then you need a "do." Take action! The Chinese have a powerful proverb that states, "I hear and I forget. I see and I remember. But I do and then I truly understand!" Remember you gotta do!

The next step is to start. This is the "art of the start!" You must begin. Make a decision then take action on your decision. My buddy Marlon Smith always ends his speeches with the following verse: "A dream without action is merely a wish. Action without a dream is merely passing time. But a dream with action can change the world!" Friends, it only takes a minute to change your life. Dream the big dream, make the decision to follow your dream, and then take action on your dream. I know for sure it will change your life!

⏰ "I Have a Dream"

Martin Luther King, Jr., gave a famous speech called "I Have A Dream." We have all heard those powerful words and his soul-stirring, passionate delivery that is timeless in its ability to inspire. In fact, no matter how often I hear that speech, I always get goose bumps because of the power that emanates from it. But as I listened I started to realize the pure importance of these four words: I-Have-a-Dream, I-Have-a-Dream. He didn't say "I had a dream," but rather "I have a dream." Why? Because to be great your dream must be ongoing. To say "I had a dream" implies that the dream has come and gone. But to have a dream means that it is ongoing, it is continuous. Do you have a dream? Is there a dream burning in your mind and spirit that consumes you and drives you to pursue it, and to eventually achieve it? I also noticed Dr. King did not say, "I have a wish." Why? Because wishes have no substance and are usually unattainable—like those who say "I wish I could live my life over again," or "I wish I were a child again." Most of us have thrown pennies into a wishing well or wished upon a star and never really expected those wishes to come true. They were just our fantasies. But a dream has substance. We dream of losing weight or buying a home or one day becoming the President of the United States. Dreams can, and do, come true! Don't be confused between a wish and a dream. Remember some people want it to happen, some wish it would happen, and others make it happen! Dream big dreams. Think big thoughts and make it happen!

Dreams are the seed for success. To make your dreams come true you must move on them, take action on them, pursue them, go after them; otherwise they are simply pipe dreams or wishes, which have no substance. A dream mixed with confidence, determination, persistence, strong desire, and action cannot be denied!

⏱ Jesse Owens, a Dreamer!

A dream mixed with confidence, determination, persistence, and strong faith is destined to become a reality. The bigger the dream, the bigger the rewards. Jesse Owens was a world-class athlete who was told that because he was African American there was no way he could compete on the same level as the German, Aryan athletes of Nazi Germany. Hitler came to the games but refused to greet this black athlete from the United

States. What Hitler did not know was that Jesse Owens was a skilled athlete who had prepared himself, but, more importantly, he was armed with a dream and great faith. The 1936 Olympics were held in Berlin. The Nazi athletes were cheered while Jesse Owens and the other American athletes were booed. Jesse did not worry about the boos or the snub by Hitler. He just concentrated on his dream. He continued to dream even after having a "foot fault" three times. He mixed his dream with his faith and on his final attempt he jumped, and won! He walked away from those Olympics with four gold medals, one for every event he participated in! A dream mixed with massive faith, confidence, and determination will always change your destiny.

A dream mixed with confidence, determination, and persistence cannot be denied, the key is that you must be willing to make a commitment to that dream and be willing to fight for the dream, if you really want it to become real in your life. In every worthwhile endeavor there will be challenges and obstacles. It is said that life gives you obstacles to see how bad you really want it. Yet when the challenges come, you must remember that you always have a choice. You can meet the challenge head-on or you can retreat and give up. The choice literally is up to you. Your commitment is what will make the difference.

◐ Commitment Creates the Magic!

When you get your dream and you start to go after that dream I can guarantee that there will be challenges. I guarantee that there will be obstacles. But if you are willing to make a commitment to your dreams and are willing to meet the challenges with a determined attitude, you will see that incredible things will start to come your way; things that would not have occurred if you had not tried. Johann Wolfgang von Goethe said it

best: "Until one is committed, there is hesitance, the chance to draw back. Always ineffectiveness. Concerning all acts of initiative (and creation), there is one elemental truth the ignorance of which kills countless ideas and splendid plans; that the moment one commits oneself, then providence moves too. All sorts of things occur to help one that would never have otherwise occurred. A whole stream of events issues from the decision, raising in one's favor all manner of unforeseen incidents and meetings and material assistance which no man could have dreamed would come his way. Whatever you can do or dream you can begin it. Boldness has genius, power and magic in it. Begin it now."

Over the last few years I have found this to be true. When you make a definite commitment to your dreams, then things happen that would never regularly have happened. I remember the day I decided to leave my job and go out on my own. It was the same day that my coworkers had laughed at me. As I was driving home that day my car started smoking and making strange noises. I stopped at a service station and asked the mechanic to look it over. He brought out a few more mechanics and he said, "Start it up," and I did. They then hit me with the news. "You need a new engine." I looked at my checkbook, which only had $200 left, and asked, "How much will that cost?" They told me it would cost approximately $3,000 and they recommended I get a new car instead. They directed me to a car dealer who was having a sale and I began the trek to the dealership.

It was the one of the longest rides I had ever taken. The car was smoking and people were honking their horns. The car was moving so slowly that I was creating a driving hazard. I was so embarrassed! Yet, on the way I had written on a piece of paper, "My goal is a brand-new car and not one penny down." I finally arrived at the dealership and went all the way around to the side entrance so they wouldn't be upset by all the smoke. I parked the car and went in. I walked into that dealership with a strange confidence because I truly believed I was going to achieve my goal of a new car without one penny down. I didn't know how, but I believed it.

A salesman came over and started showing me the new models and I looked, and looked, and looked until I saw the one I wanted . . . the luxury model. Then he hit me with the lines that would test my resolve. "What do you have for collateral?" I mumbled, "A 280Z sports car." He said, "Great! Let's go test-drive it!" All that I could do at that moment was to take a deep breath, give him the keys and start to PRAY! He walked out to the car, opened the door, and stuck the key in the ignition.

At that moment something strange happened. The ignition wouldn't turn. He had jammed the ignition switch! He tried and tried; and I even tried, then he got the head mechanic, who also tried and tried and tried. Finally they said they couldn't get the key to work, but that the car *looked* good, so they were willing to make me an offer. I left the lot that day with a brand-new car, not one penny down, and the complimentary seat covers to go with it!

What were the chances of that happening at that moment? I do not know the probability, but I believe that it would be zero if I had given up when the guy told me I needed a new engine. The probability for success would have been zero if I had turned around and gone back and begged for my old job and had not tried. Commitment really does have magic in it!

But, there is more to this story. The next morning I woke up and realized that in the excitement of the moment I had lost track of the fact that I had left the dealer with a lemon, a car with a broken engine. I knew I could not start off this new career, where I speak to people about integrity and character, with this kind of situation. I got up and drove back to the dealership and walked up to the sales manager and handed him the key. I told him "Sir, with all the excitement of yesterday I did not realize I left you with a car that had a broken engine. Here is your car back. I apologize for any inconvenience. Please send me a bill for any mileage that I accumulated." He was stunned and looked at me as if he had seen a ghost. He said, "I can't believe you would come back! I can't believe it!'' He then went on to say, ''My friend, I want to thank you for coming back and offering the car back, but that's not necessary. See, your car didn't have a broken engine . . . it just needed some oil!'' He went on to refer me to others and to recommend me as a speaker who walks, or should I say drives, his talk!

Commitment! Commitment is the key when you go out after your dreams because life will test you to see how badly you really want it! This poem captures the Goethe verse on commitment!

> *Whatever you can do, or dream you can do,*
> *begin it*
> *Boldness has power and magic and genius in*
> *it*
> *Decide and begin and the mind grows heated*
> *Then believe and proceed, and the task will be*
> *completed!*

⏱ The No-Option Person

We talked about how you have to give your all when you want to reach your goal; you have to be completely focused on your goal; you have to become a "no-option person." A "no-option person" has no other options: he or she has to make it or else; do or die, all or nothing! When you become that committed, you will make it happen because you have no other choice! There was a general who took his troops to a major battle on an a distant shore. As they approached the enemy he saw that they were outnumbered, and his troops were afraid because the enemy seemed so big and strong. But the general knew they had the potential to win. After they hit land he saw the fear and how the men were tentative in advancing, so he gave the order to "Burn the boats." They now had no other choices, no other options; they had to win or die. At that moment his troops became energized and fearless, because they had no other options. They fought and gave their all, and they won. We must develop a sink-or-swim, "no-option" mind-set, a do-or-die attitude. We have to make it happen. If you do, if you make that kind of commitment, then your dreams will come true, in fact they must come true! Why? Because you have no other option!

Friends, you have power in your dreams. But you must activate the power by making the decision to follow your dreams.

> *Power is yours if you let it go.*
> *If you let it show.*
> *If you let it flow!*
> *Just give it a start*
> *With all of your heart*
> *Give your best shot*
> *And it will never part*
> *You've got the power!*

Friends, remember that there will be challenges and there will be difficulties but *you* must make the choice as to whether you let them keep you from your goal. Or you can let them push you towards your goal! The old saying goes, "Obstacles are really opportunities in work clothes!" Do not be discouraged by obstacles; just remember that commitment has magic and genius in it. Begin it NOW!

It sounds elementary, it sounds simple, but that does not mean that it is easy. It is not easy! It is difficult because we first have to overcome the negative seeds that have been planted in our minds over the span of our lifetimes. In discussing success, Les Brown shared with me that the hard part of his success was not making a million dollars! The hardest part was simply believing that it was possible that he could make a million dollars!

My son and I were riding by the building where I used to work, where my coworkers stood at the door and laughed at me. My son, who was about eight years old at the time, asked, "Daddy, isn't that where you used to work?" I said, "Yes." He said, "Daddy, did you get fired?" I answered, "No, I quit!" When I said that I could see the pain etched on his face because he has heard me say millions of times, "Never give up, never give up, no matter what, never give up!" I stopped the car and looked him in the eye and told him, **"William, I QUIT ... not because I was giving up, but because I *WAS GOING UP*!"**

Sometimes you have to quit things that keep you down, keep you bound, and make you frown. You have to realize that to do the incredible, you must first dream the impossible. Dream! Then make the decision to act on your dreams with positive, determined action. Pursue excellence in all that you do. Develop great desire and commitment to reach your dreams. Then take full responsibility for your success. Get serious, and in short order you will see your dreams sprout, grow, and blossom! Dream the impossible! Go forth and be bold!

⏱ Two Choices?

Today's Motivational Minute is taken from the tape series of James Anthony Carter, "The Unstoppable Visionary." Mr. Carter states, "Creativity and living are not without their difficulties. The unfortunate thing about having a dream is that nobody believes in it, initially, but you. But when the dream comes true, they'll all say that it was obvious all along. This being the case, you have two choices in life. Listen to the naysayers or follow your dream." Since you are reading this Motivational Minute, you have taken a step toward your dream. You have chosen to be different; you have chosen to be yourself! And in choosing to be yourself you have chosen to be that which the creator meant for you to be. Friends, dream big dreams, think big thoughts, because dreams can and do come true. Robert F. Kennedy said it so well when he noted, "Some men see

things as they are and ask, Why? I dream things that never were and ask, Why not?" I ask you to dream big dreams, in fact impossible dreams, and continue to ask "Why not?" Remember that all things are possible if you can just believe!

CHAPTER III

Goals:
Dreams with a Deadline!

One of the questions I regularly get asked is, "What is the difference between dreams and goals?" Well, goals are an outgrowth of your dreams. They are the stepping-stones to your dreams. A goal is simply a dream with a deadline. Let's say that your dream is to go to law school. A goal is when you commit to a time period in which you are going to make this dream into a reality. You have now focused the dream and made it into your goal.

The renowned Zig Ziglar has a great analogy that talks about focus, where he says that a magnifying glass can ignite a fire on a pile of leaves if you concentrate the power of the sun through the glass at a focussed, specific spot and do not move the glass. Goals help to focus your dreams and make you specify WHEN you want to achieve them. They are stepping-stones to make your dreams come true. The key is to dream big dreams, think big thoughts, and then transform those dreams into attainable, reachable goals and ACT!

☽ A Goal: A Target

How do you make your dreams come true? First, you have to know what your dreams are. If I gave you a ball

and told you to hit a ten-foot wall that was five feet in front of you, could you do it? Of course, no problem! But if I blindfolded you and took you five steps back and then twirled you around ten times would you still be able to hit the wall with ease? No! It is difficult to hit what you can't see, and it is impossible to hit what you don't know! That is why you must set goals. The starting point for your goals are your dreams. A goal is nothing more than a dream with a deadline. What is your dream and what is your goal?

What is your goal? What are your dreams for this year? What are your goals for this year? What do you want to accomplish in the next twelve months? Let's do an exercise to help you to focus on your goals. Take a piece of paper and write the numbers from one to ten in list form. Now I want you to think, what would you go after if you were guaranteed that you could not fail? What would you attempt, what would you try to accomplish if you were told that it was impossible for you to fail? Think like a child on Christmas morning. Anything you want, you can achieve. Anything. Write down at least ten things; if you have more, write them down, too. Do not limit yourself by your present circumstances. Anything you want, you can accomplish; it is now impossible for you to fail.

Once you have made your list, you have taken the first step to success. Make copies of that list and read it every day. Read it and reread it until you believe it. Then read it some more. Keep on reading it and start acting on it and you will be amazed at how many things you will start to accomplish. In the movie *The Ten Commandments*, there is a line that I always remember: "So as it is written, so shall it be done!" Write your dreams and set the goals, and remember, "So as it is written, so shall it be done!"

⏰ The DreamSheet

The reason we completed the exercise above was that it will help us determine our dreams and goals (because we realize that it is impossible to hit a target you cannot see and that you do not know). You made a list of at least ten things you would go after this year if you knew that it was impossible for you to fail. Now that your mind is in the possibility mode, let's go a step further. I want you to take out four sheets of paper. On the first sheet write, "My lifetime dreams and goals." On the second sheet write, "My twelve-month dreams and goals." On the third sheet write, "My thirty-day goals," and on the fourth sheet write "My ideal successful daily routine."

Once you have developed a routine for a successful day, then the key to success is simply to reproduce that successful day seven times and you have a successful week, then reproduce that successful week four times and you have a successful month, and reproduce that successful month twelve times and you have a successful year. And you are then on your way to creating a successful lifetime! But it all starts with a dream and a goal. Do this exercise right now, and don't limit your dreams by your present circumstances. Remember, you are guaranteed success; it is impossible for you to fail. Just believe!

The DreamBuilding Formula

1. Decide what you want
2. Write it down (be specific)
3. Read it three times a day
4. Set the date of accomplishment
5. Think of it often
6. Dream and imagine (see yourself enjoying it)
7. Develop a plan of action
8. Do three things every day towards the goal
9. Stay positive (read and listen to positive things daily)
10. Act as though you have achieved it (conceive-believe-achieve)

Not long ago, while I was stuck in a small town due to inclement weather, I was flipping channels and happened upon a documentary on martial arts legend Bruce Lee. I was extremely interested in him because I remember as a child how much I liked his character, Kato, in *The Green Hornet* television show. I sat up and looked at the documentary and was highly impressed with the information I received. Bruce Lee was born in San Francisco but his family moved back to China while he was a small child. He grew up learning the martial arts and acting and found a way to combine his two loves into a unique artistic expression. He came back to America and began to teach his new artistic form of karate. During his struggling days he wrote a "major aim" sheet, which detailed his lifetime goals and dreams. His top-priority goal was to be the highest paid and best known Asian actor and martial artist of all times.

He struggled for a while after the cancellation of *The Green Hornet* and soon he went back to China, where he began making martial arts movies. The movies became hits and he became a major success in China. The same producers and movie makers who had turned him down in America were now calling and making him offers. He was such a big star everywhere else that he was able to leverage his popularity into a contract that made him the highest paid Asian artist of all times. Shortly after finishing *Enter the Dragon* he died from hypersensitivity to a pain reliever, yet he had reached his goal and "major aim." His stardom continued after his death with a hit movie and a star on the Hollywood Walk of Fame!

The main point to take from this story is that life is very unpredictable and there's not a lot to depend on except your dreams and your faith. If you can dream, believe in those dreams, go after those dreams, set goals (or in this case major aims), then you can do incredible things! As Bruce Lee proved, dreams can come true!

There was one quote from that Bruce Lee movie that made an indelible impression on me. He said, "When I came over on the boat, I knew that this was an 'idea place.'

A man with an idea and desire can do anything!'' Friends, this truly is an "idea place." I implore you to dream big dreams, think big thoughts, let your mind soar and create new ideas. And you will see that dreams can, and do, come true!

⏱ Scott McKain and His Buddy Arnold

Scott McKain is a gifted speaker, author, and television host who I was privileged to share the speaking stage with. Scott tells a story about Arnold Schwarzenegger that shows the power of dreams and goals. As a young man growing up in Austria, Arnold Schwarzenegger made up his mind that he was going to do some incredible things with his life. He made up his mind and set a goal to be the greatest bodybuilder of all time. Many thought Arnold was crazy but they figured he would eventually give up, because it would take a great deal of time and commitment. They figured he would give up and get over that silly notion, and get a "real" job. He then added another aspect to his dream, he not only wanted to become the world's greatest bodybuilder but he also wanted to become a movie star and an international fitness guru! His friends said, "What a crazy dream!" He wrote his dreams down on a note card and carried it around in his wallet and made a contract with himself that he would achieve this goal. He said it was this contract with himself that drove him, forced him, to go to America and start the climb to become Mr. Olympia. He went on to become one of the highest paid actors in Hollywood and the Chairman of the President's Committee for Physical Fitness. Do dreams and goals make a difference? You'd better believe it, just ask Arnold!

⏱ Resolutions, or Just a Waste of Time?

Many people make lots of New Year's resolutions. The problem is these usually only last a couple of weeks. Statistics show that the sale of diet products and health club attendance are highest in the first two weeks of the year. People are motivated on the first days of January and are really into their resolutions, but that enthusiasm starts to dwindle by the fifteenth of the month, and usually fizzles out by the end of the month. Why? Because of a lack of continuous and constant motivation. They get motivated at the first of the year but don't keep it up. Some people say the problem with motivation is that it wears off. Well, so does eating and bathing; yet part of your daily routine is to eat and to bathe. To make your resolutions into realities it is essential that you make motivation a part of your daily routine, to read or listen to something motivational, to fill your mind with that which is positive and encouraging. Find something (a book, a tape, or music) that encourages and inspires you to dream and then motivates you to go after your dreams. I recommend that you make this, the Magnificent Motivational Minute, a part of your daily routine. It will help you to grow, help you to focus, and help you to stay motivated. Ladies and gentlemen, remember that it only takes a minute to change your life. If you invest in yourself you will see results in an amazing amount of time. Make a resolution to stay motivated this year. Have a Great Day and a Great Year!

⏱ California or Bust!

What is the essential ingredient that can propel a person to success? What is the special key that can unlock untold doors? What is the tool that can help mold your future? Well, it's simple yet greatly misused and misunderstood. It is a goal. A goal is a dream with a time frame attached to it. Goals are stepping-stones to reach our dreams. If we can concentrate on goals, learn how to set them and how to reach them, we can reach exceptional heights. The pioneers during the Gold Rush had the goal of reaching California. They had a saying: "California or bust!" They had a dream, set a time to achieve it, and made a commitment to reach their goal or else. We must make the same commitment to reach our goals and then do it. This is one of my favorite sayings: "It is the carrot in front of the horse's face that makes it want to run the race!" Run fast and run hard and enjoy the rewards that are set in front of your face!

⏱ Do Not Change Your Decision to Go, Change Your Direction!

You've got your dream. You've set your goal. You're ready to get started and then you encounter difficulty. Don't change your decision to go, just change your path to get there! Numerous paths can lead to each goal. For example, if you're on your way to work and you come to a street that is closed, do you give up and go back home? No! You find another street that's open or another route to get to work. With your goal, if you encounter difficulty, don't change your decision to go; change your direction to get there.

⏱ The Difference Between a Goal and a Vision

Earlier I told you that dreams are the seed for success. And after you have identified the dream, you must break the dream down into achievable chunks called "goals." Goals are dreams on a deadline. Yet there is another level that must be achieved in the dream process. After you get your dream and you have implemented the goal-setting process to help you to achieve those dreams, then you must go to the next level, which is creating a vision. A vision is a dream where you can actually see yourself in the dream, almost as if it were already a reality. To continue to dream dreams that are of visionary status, you must start the process of becoming a visionary. A *visionary* is one who habitually dreams big dreams that become visions, and habitually makes those dreams become realities. A dream leads to a goal, which leads to the achievement of the dream, which then leads to more dreams, which leads to becoming a visionary. What is the difference between a goal and a vision? A goal is something that you have, while a vision is something that has you! A goal is not just something you work on, but it becomes something that works on you, not so much what you get but what you become in the process. Thoreau said: "In the long run people only hit what they aim at. Therefore, they ought to aim high." Friends, dream big dreams, aim high; and work on BECOMING A VISIONARY.

Remember:

> Whatever you can do, or dream you can do,
>   begin it;
> Boldness has power and magic and genius in
>   it;
> Just begin and the mind grows heated;
> Then believe and proceed, and the task will be
>   completed!

56

CHAPTER IV

As a Man Thinketh!

"So as a man thinketh in his heart, so as he is" (Proverbs 23:7). For many years I heard this scripture, but I had no real understanding of its meaning. I thought that in life you were just supposed to go with the flow. And what happened, or did not happen, was just the way it was supposed to be. Those who were successful were just lucky. I went with the flow, and most times I was like a ship lost in the storm, getting tossed from here to there, from there to here, and constantly lost and without focus. Then I started to realize that I have some personal responsibility for my success and that my thinking determined my actions. I reread the verse over and over again and came to see that it was not just the thinking in my head but also the thinking in my heart. Why? Because my heart contained my true core beliefs—the beliefs that determine what I really think and therefore what I will attempt and what I will be able to achieve!

Why does it say, "As he thinketh in his heart"? Well, what we think in our head can be quite different from what we think in our heart. Motivation deals with our heads. Its job is to get us to take action, to get up and do something. Inspiration deals with our hearts, the inner person. It really does not care what our heads have to say! The head may say that what we plan to do is illogical, impossible, and cannot be done, but the heart does not care and ignores the head and the logic of the issue and goes after what it "feels" it must do. We often hear of people who were inspired to achieve impossible feats. There are athletes who dedicate a game to a fallen friend or family member and do things that they never knew they could do; or stories of accident or disaster victims who exhibit superhuman strength to rescue others. As people thinketh in their hearts, so as they are!

⏰ The Real You

When you look in the mirror, you see a face that you have known all your life. You see a person that you intimately connect with. You see you! But it is not the real you, the true you. The real you is on the inside, the inner person. And that inner person is directly responsible for the outer you and the things you do or don't do. As a man thinketh in his heart, his core, his true being, so as he is! The inner you is the core you. Just as the heart of the artichoke is the prime part, your core is your best part. The core of the apple is the most important part because after all is said and done (or in this case, after all is said and eaten), the core contains the seeds that are the future of that apple. If you cut an apple in half you could count the seeds in that apple. But you could not count the future apples that are in those seeds!

The center, the core, of the pineapple is where the sweetest fruit is found. The same is true for us. The heart is the core, where our most intense thoughts, feelings, and beliefs are found. If you can tap into that inner person and tap into the thoughts and feelings that are found there, then you can begin to tap into your "true thoughts, dreams, beliefs, and values." These are the things that make you *act* on your desires. These are the things that guide, direct, determine, and create how you live your life. This is where you determine what you will and will not do, what you go after and what you choose to ignore, what you attempt and what you shy away from. As a man thinketh in his heart, in his core, his inner man, so as he is. The core, the center, the heart is the real you.

⏰ Change Your Thinking

Before you change your thinking, you have to change what goes into your mind. To change where you're going you must first change your thinking. Your thinking affects how you act and therefore what you do, just as to change your weight and health you must change what you eat. And the same is true for your mind. You must fill your mind with positive, healthy, inspirational, and encouraging material and get rid of the things that will kill your dreams and aspirations: doubt, fear, and negative thinking. Just as you are what you eat, you also are exactly what you think about. Remember that your input always determines your output. Change your thinking and change your life!

⏰ Great Thinkers

Great thinkers throughout history have had many different philosophies of life, but all agree on the fact that success is a direct result of your thinking. Dr. Norman Vincent Peale said, "If you think in negative terms you would get negative results. Yet if you could think in positive terms, you would achieve positive results." Ralph Waldo Emerson said, "A man is what he thinks about all day long." William James, the great philosopher and psychologist, said, "My greatest discovery in human beings is that they can alter their lives by altering their attitudes of mind." Dr. Ben Carson, author of *Gifted Hands* and a renowned neurosurgeon, said,

"Think big, think bold, think stretch, think global, think quantum leap!" Finally, the carpenter from Galilee, the greatest positive thinker of all time, said, "If you can just believe, all things are possible to those who believe." Folks, you can if you think you can. As a man thinketh . . . so as he is! Think great thoughts, do great things, and have a great day!

⏲ The Mind Tattoo

Dr. Norman Vincent Peale stated: "If you think in negative terms, you will get negative results. Yet if you think in positive terms, you will get positive results." His book *The Power of Positive Thinking* became the standard for a new generation of positive thinkers. In fact, it was one of the first books that I read as I made the transition from a negative reactor to a positive creator. I started to realize I could create some of my circumstances by having a positive mental attitude. I once heard a powerful story that Dr. Peale shared on a television show. He told of how he had been walking by a tattoo shop and a very confused-looking man came out of the shop with a new tattoo on his arm that read "Born to Lose!" Dr. Peale watched the man stumble down the street and then noticed that the tattoo artist had come out of the shop and also looked as the man walked away. Dr. Peale asked the tattoo artist about the young man with the "Born to Lose" tattoo. The old tattoo artist sadly shook his head and said, "I asked him if he was sure that he wanted the tattoo to state that he was born to lose. And he was adamant that he did." Dr. Peale said, "Isn't that strange?" Then the tattoo artist said, "Not really! See, before he had it tattooed on his arm, he had tattooed it on his brain!" He believes that he really was born to lose and therefore he will act like he was born to lose. None of us were born to lose. We were born to win! But the choice is up to us!

⏱ You Can Lead a Horse to Water, But . . .

You can lead a horse to water, but you can't make him drink. You can take a fool to wisdom, but can't make him think. There is a story about a man who was looking for the secret to success. He came to a wise man and asked, "What do I have to do to become a success?" The wise man said, "You have to change your thinking and change what you do and change how you act and finally you have to be willing to make some sacrifices." The young man paused to reflect on the wise man's words, and then he walked away. He didn't want to change his thinking and didn't want to stop doing what he was doing. He didn't want to make the necessary sacrifices because it would be uncomfortable. Many have heard what it takes to be successful but refuse to change and therefore choose to fail. Ladies and gentlemen, it's as old as time. You are what you think about. Change your thinking and change your life!

We become what we think about. How you think determines what you do and what goals you will go after. Those who think about a definite goal are more likely to reach that goal, while those who think about nothing tend to do nothing. Those who have no idea where they are going have thoughts of confusion, doubt, and fear. Since that is what they think about, that is usually what they get: lives filled with confusion, anxiety, and doubt. If you think about nothing, you tend to do nothing; if you think about great things, you are more apt to do great things.

⏱ The Poison Mushroom

To become a success you must be careful what you allow to enter your mind, because your mind is like a garden. It will grow whatever is planted. If you plant positive it will grow positive, but if you plant negative you will grow negative. If you plant corn it will grow

61

corn, but if you plant poison mushrooms then they, too, will grow; in fact, weeds and other undesirable plants tend to grow quicker, and tend to choke and overtake other plants. That is why you must be careful what you allow to enter in your mind, because it will grow. As you sow so shall you reap. Think about nothing and you will do nothing: think about great things and you will do great things. Think positive and you will grow positive, think negative and you will grow negative!

🕐 Make It a Winning Life

Every day is a great day, and even if it doesn't feel like a great day you can make it a great day. My friend Wolf Rinke, author of *Make It a Winning Life: Success Strategies for Life, Love and Business*, says that life is essentially what you make it and that you must make things happen for yourself. You make every day a great day by programming your mind that it is a great day. Psychiatrists state that most illnesses are psychosomatic, which means that your mind creates them. We all know people who, no matter what kind of illness you might mention, have either had that condition or are having it right then. There is a definite relationship between the psyche, which is your mind, and the soma, which is your body. Just as your mind creates the illness in your body, studies show that if you program your mind with positive rather than negative information, the mind can create an exhilarating and exceptional day, every day. Every day can be a great day and your life can be a winning life, if you are willing to make it that way! Think great thoughts, do great things, and make it a winning day!

🕐 Insanity?

To change where you are, you must change your thinking. Your thinking not only determines where you are today, but, more importantly, where you are going tomorrow. If you want success it is imperative that you change your thinking because the definition of "insanity" is to keep on doing exactly what you've been doing in the exact same way and expect different results! You've got to change your thinking! If you can change *how you think*, you will change *how you act*. And if you can change *how you act*, you will change *what you do*. And if you can change *what you do*, then you will change *what you get*. And if you can change *what you get*, you will change *where you're going*. And if you can change *where you're going*, you will *change your life*! Change your thinking and change your life!

🕐 Go With the Flow?

"If it is to be, then it is up to me." We've all heard this saying. But what does it really mean? Well, it means we must take responsibility for our success or our failure. We must either act on life or life will act on us. We can either go with the flow, which may take us any old place, or we can direct the flow and therefore determine our destination. If you look at boats sailing on a river, you will notice that if the wind is blowing south, some boats will go with the flow and travel south. Yet there will also be boats that are going north, east, and west. They are not going with the flow but rather are using the flow to go where they want to go. You determine where you want to go in life. It may not be easy to go where there is no path, but if you do you'll be the trailblazer.

Your thinking determines how you act and what you do, which determines what you get, and what you get determines where you go. It sounds so simple. Yet I often wonder why I didn't change my thinking earlier. And since I was able to change my thinking, why don't others simply change theirs? The reason is that even though it sounds simple, it isn't easy. Someone said, "You are where you are and what you are because of what goes into your mind, which creates your thinking."

I remember when I was a full-time musician, one of my friends told me to "go with the flow, go with what's going good." It sounded so cool and hip that I accepted it as my philosophy, even though what was "going good" may not have been what I really wanted to do or where I really wanted to go. In fact, what I thought of as living well was really a mirage. I was so far behind that I thought I was in front!

For example, once I was offered a job that I really did not want. But I figured, "Go with what's going, go with the flow" (even though it wasn't where I really wanted to go). I hated the job and it literally made me sick, but I stayed because they kept paying me. I now realize how backward that thinking was. In fact, it is the way many people think. Statistics show that more than 80 percent of all Americans go to jobs they really cannot stand. I know that's true because I was one of them, a backward thinker! You could say the way I was thinking was so backward that if you took my brain and put it in a bird, that bird would take off and fly backward!

Once I changed my thinking, I started to read about others who had decided to do what they wanted to do and to use the flow to go where they wanted to go. I read about others who realized that you must change your thinking in order to change your life. Otherwise you remain the same, at the same place, doing the same thing, and getting the same results. As Zig Ziglar says, "You gotta change that stinking thinking!"

⏰ The Small-Minded Fisherman

To have big achievements you must have big dreams and big goals. You should never settle for your present circumstances. Instead, you should always reach higher. There is a story about a fisherman who caught fish with such ease that it was amazing. But as he caught the fish he did something strange—he kept the little ones and threw the big ones back. Someone asked him why he did this, and he answered, "Because I only have a little pan!" Ladies and gentlemen, our reach should always exceed our grasp.

⏰ The Creative-Thinking Fisherman

We talked about how many people let their circumstances and their situations limit what they think they can achieve. I shared the story about the shortsighted fisherman who kept the little fish and threw the big ones back because he had a little pan. Well, to go one step further, not only was he shortsighted, but due to his limited vision and lack of imagination, he was unable to take advantage of obvious opportunities. His vision was so limited that he could not think of other options to reach his goal. The problem was not the size of the pan but rather the size of his thinking. Little thinking always gets little results, because little thinking will limit the possibilities that exist. The fisherman could have simply cut the fish into smaller pieces, rather than throwing the fish back! Far too many of us let our present circumstances stop us, and shackle our creativity. To make your dreams come true you must be creative and allow you mind to soar, as it was meant to do. Remember, you can, if you think you can!

🕐 The Ole Country Dog

Most people don't live their dreams because they are afraid and they don't want to take any chances. They would rather sit around, complain, and bemoan their state than to live their dreams. They let life determine where they are going. Like the old saying, "If you don't know where you're going, any road will do." Well, if you don't know who you are, you'll answer to any name. Did you know that the number one time for people to have heart attacks is between 7 and 9 on Monday mornings? This is the time when people have to get up and go to jobs that they hate, jobs they can't stand. Then they sit around and complain all day long. Ladies and gentlemen, you should never complain about what you allow. You have a choice!

Let me share a story with you that illustrates this point. There was a man walking down a country road. He walked past a porch, where an old farmer was sitting in his rocking chair, and next to him was a dog that was howling and making all sorts of noise. So the man walked up to the farmer and said, "Why is that dog howling and making so much noise?" The farmer said, "Because he's sitting on a nail." And the man said, "Why doesn't he get up?" and the farmer said, " 'Cause it don't hurt bad enough!" If you go to a job you can't stand and all you do is sit around and complain, then you're no better than that old dog sitting on a nail. Ladies and gentlemen, don't complain about what you allow. You have a choice. You should choose where you want to go in life. You can, if you want to! Choose to be Great!

🕐 Decide to Be Happy!

I saw a commercial on television that features a senior citizen who said she had two choices every morning! She could choose to be happy or she could choose to

66

be sad. She said she chooses to be happy because happiness is a choice. You can wake up with a bad attitude or you can wake up with a good attitude. Every day is a brand-new opportunity and how you receive it is up to you. Some people wake up with a positive attitude and a positive state of mind and say "Good morning, Lord," while others wake up with a negative attitude and a negative state of mind and say, "Good Lord, it's morning!" Whatever perspective you choose is up to you. I suggest that you wake up and say "Good morning, Lord," because every day you wake up truly is a good morning (as Zig Ziglar says, "If you don't believe it . . . just try missing one"). When you wake up, simply count your blessings and choose to be happy. It truly is your choice!

⏱ Growing Pains

Most people don't live life to the fullest because they have fear. They let fear rob them of life and the joys of living. I don't want you to be reckless and foolish, but I do want you to take chances and challenge yourself, for if you're afraid to take some risks you will never grow, never stretch, never reach your potential. You've got to be willing to stretch, to grow, to push yourself. Sometimes it will be painful but there is no growth without pain. That's why they're called growing pains.

What would you think if you had a baby who was three years old and had not grown from infancy? You'd rush it to the doctor. Or suppose the baby fell down once and just stopped trying to walk? You'd say there is something wrong because you know that without falling and getting back up the baby would never learn to walk. We cannot stop trying just because we fall or just because it is painful. Growth is painful, but it is necessary. This is a quote from the families of the astronauts who died in the tragic *Challenger* shuttle disaster: "Do not fear risk; all exploration, all growth is calculated. Life is filled with challenge. Only those who are willing to go after those challenges grow. Only if we are willing to walk over the edge can we become winners." Remember, all things are possible if you can just believe.

⏱ Yes I Can!

If you want to be successful, if you want to make your dreams into realities, you have to change your thinking. You have to develop your thinking to the point where you honestly believe that it is impossible for you to fail. A few years ago there was a great football game between the Houston Oilers and the Buffalo Bills. The Houston Oilers were ahead at half-time, 35–3, and Buffalo had its second-string quarterback in. Everybody was just hoping that the game would be over soon to put the Bills out of their misery. But the Bills didn't doubt their ability or that they could win the game. They came out the second half and scored 38 points and won the game 41–38! This example clearly illustrates that to be a winner you must think like a winner.

This poem is a well-known standard that has passed the test of time. The author remains unknown, but the impact remains unwavering.

> *If you think you are beaten, you are,*
> *If you think you dare not, you don't.*
> *If you like to win but you think you can't,*
> *It's almost a cinch you won't.*
> *If you think you'll lose, you've lost.*
> *For in this world you will surely find*
> *Success being with a person's will,*
> *It's all in the state of mind.*
> *Think Big and your deeds will grow,*
> *Think small and you'll fall behind.*

Think that you can and you will,
It's all in the state of mind.
If you think you're outclassed, you are,
You have to think big to rise.
You've got to be sure of yourself,
Before you can win the prize.
Life's battles don't always go,
To the strongest woman or man,
But sooner or later the person who wins
Is the person who thinks they can!

⏲ It Doesn't Matter!

Wally Amos, the famous cookie man, shared with me that far too many people major in the minors and minor in the majors. They concentrate on things that really don't matter. He said that when you look at a newspaper obituary you see the year a person was born and the year they died. And it will be separated by a dash, i.e. 1900–1996. Most people will concentrate on when the person was born or when they died. But that is not nearly as important as what they did in between, in the dash! What's in the dash? Friends, it's doesn't matter how much money you have. It doesn't matter your gender or your color of skin. Because in the end, it's your attitude that lets you win! You can if you think you can! What will go in *your* dash?

⏲ CDI (Can Do It)

Not long ago I started a club called CDI, which means the "Can Do It" club. We help people to develop the mental attitude that they can do it, no matter what it is they are trying to accomplish. First they must think they can do it. CDI members have a strong belief in the fact that even if they do not get it the first time, they will keep trying because . . . they can do it!

You, Too, Can Do It!
You Can Learn It, You Can Earn It
You Can Aspire To It, You Can Desire It
You Can Confront It, You Can Defeat It
You Can Design It, You Can Build It
You Can Make It, You Can Mold It
You Can Grasp It, You Can Hold It
You Can Conceive It, You Can Achieve
    It
You Can Believe It, You Can Receive It
You Can Do It . . . CDI, You Can Do
    It!

🕐 **Bargained with Life for a Penny**

Another great day. That's right, another great day! It is another great day because you determine whether today will be great or miserable. You determine whether you will be a success or a failure. You determine what you get out of life by what you put into life. Most people receive not and achieve not because they ask not and believe not. Most people settle for the leftovers that life gives them rather than going out and eating from the banquet table of life's successes. This poem illustrates this point.

> *I Bargained with Life for a Penny,*
> *And Life Would Pay No More,*
> *However I Begged at Evening,*
> *When I Counted My Scanty Store.*
> *For Life Is a Just Employer,*
> *And Gives You What You Ask,*
> *But Once You Have Set the*
>   *Wages,*
> *Why, Then You Must Bear the*
>   *Task.*

> *I Worked for a Menial Hire,*
> *Only to Learn Dismayed,*
> *That Any Wage I Had Asked Life*
> *   for,*
> *Life Would Have Gladly Paid.*
>
> AUTHOR UNKNOWN

Friends, stop settling for pennies when you can have dollars. Dream big dreams, think big thoughts, and you can have your heart's desire.

⏱ Settling for the Leftovers

We spoke of how most people settle in life for the leftovers life gives rather than creating for themselves a banquet table. They dream little dreams, think little thoughts, and get little results. Why? Because most don't think they can do any better. They settle for mediocrity rather than going the extra steps for excellence. They don't think they can do it. And if you think you can or think you can't, either way you're probably right. You accomplish what you think you can accomplish. You can if you think you can and you probably won't if you think you can't. Most people simply won't try! They go to their graves with their dreams still inside of them. Well, in America there is no excuse for failure. You live in one of the greatest countries in the world. It's a country with unbelievable opportunities, and most of us act like the man who was told to go into a bank and take whatever he wanted. He took a penny and left because he didn't think he could handle any more! He thought it would be too hard to keep the wealth. Ladies and gentlemen, we are what we think about. Think big!

⏰ It Does Not Matter Where You Come From

We talked before about the story of the man who went into the bank and was told to take whatever he wanted and he took but a penny because he didn't think he could handle any more. To be in America and not to take advantage of the opportunities is to be like that man. Did you know that a person from another country becomes a millionaire in the U.S. five times faster than someone who is born here? Why? Because they want it more! Many come from countries with limited opportunities, countries where they might only be able to earn five dollars a week. They come to America where they can make five dollars in just an hour and often they work two or three or four jobs. Ladies and gentlemen, they do whatever is necessary to make their dreams come true. Immigrants come to this country, see all the opportunities, and then they make it happen, while many of us are still sitting around crying, whining, and complaining. There is no shortage of money. There is only a shortage of ideas and desire. Dream bigger dreams, think bigger thoughts, and make it a great day and a great life.

⏰ An Immigrant Attitude!

What is an immigrant attitude? Well it is an attitude that I learned about the hard way. Not long ago I spent the weekend with Les Brown and Gladys Knight. While there I was asked to join them for a game of tennis. They already had a foursome but there was a fifth person in the group who they asked me to play with. This gentleman was about sixty-five years old, had white hair, and had a pronounced limp, which seemed to be the result of a earlier stroke. We started hitting and he asked if I wanted to play. I said that would be fine, but I wasn't planning on exerting myself, because he was an old man who had a bad leg.

We played and soon got to the point where we both had won four games and had only two games to go to finish the set. I figured he probably had not won a game in a long time so I let him win. I figured that would be all and he would be ready to leave. But he then said he wanted to also win the second set so he could have a complete match. What?! He wanted to win a second set? I let him win, and now he wanted a match? No way! I decided it was time to stop fooling around and really play. Very quickly I won five straight games and as we were changing sides the old gentleman said, "Young man, you only have one game to go, but I'm going to win! See, I am an immigrant and this is the position I like to be in!" I laughed and told him he was definitely hallucinating. An hour later we left that court. . . . And the old gentleman had won!

Les laughed when I shared the story with him. I noted that we usually learn more in failure than we do in success. I learned a valuable lesson that day on that tennis court. I learned about an immigrant attitude. Immigrants come to this country with a different kind of attitude. They like being the underdog and actually believe they are going to win. They see this as the land of opportunity and they see Americans as people who usually do not take advantage of the opportunities.

From that experience I made up my mind that I was going to develop an immigrant attitude! I made up my mind to win in spite of the circumstances and to take advantage of the opportunities that this country offers. I say that you, too, should develop this same kind of attitude, whether you were born in America or not. Develop an immigrant attitude and decide to win!

⏰ No Shortage of Millionaires

Millionaire, millionaire, we hear the word often but we have misconceptions about millionaires. I told you that there is no shortage of money in America but rather a shortage of ideas and a shortage of dreams and desire. That still might not strike home until you realize that there is no shortage of money. Statistics show that a new millionaire is created in America approximately every fifty-eight minutes. Every fifty-eight minutes! There is no shortage of money, only a shortage of ideas and a shortage of desire, real desire to go after your dreams. Friends, we have to go after our dreams and determine in our minds and in our hearts that we will not stop until we reach our goals. Our dreams and goals should always exceed our reach. We must expand our visions of ourselves, broaden how we perceive ourselves, and we've got to stretch, leave our comfort zones, and make those dreams come true.

🕐 If You Think You Can

If you think you can or think you can't . . . you are probably right. It's an old saying but it is a profound one that never loses its truth. I know from personal experience. I have found that when I think I can I tend to have a much higher success rate than when I think I can't. Why? Because when I think I can I at least will try. When I made up my mind to change my life, I had to make a conscious decision to think that I could, that it was possible to change. First, I convinced myself that I could make a change. Then I started preparing myself for my new life. How? I developed a love of reading, a habit of reading more books and specifically self-development/self-help books and biographies. I read about other people and by so doing I reprogrammed my mind. I developed a mind-set that said, "If they can do it, then I can do it." It just depended on how badly I wanted it. I started being exposed to other people who had overcome obstacles and had made a conscious effort to overcome their limiting circumstances. I realized I had talents I was not even using, because I didn't think I could. I went from small achievements to bigger achievements, then on to bigger and bigger and bigger achievements, because I started not only think that I could but, more important, to actually believe it. And I found it to be true that all things are possible if you can just believe!

⏱ If They Can, So Can I!

We are what we think about. Throughout history we have seen countless examples of people who have changed their lives and their circumstances by changing their thinking. We have heard about those who have programmed their minds to believe that they could, when all around them said that they couldn't. They have developed the faith to overcome impossible situations because they put in their minds that it was impossible to fail. Among them are Mary McLeod Bethune, who started a college with six dollars to her name; Jesse Owens, who won four gold medals after Hitler said it was impossible; Helen Keller, who was born deaf and blind; Dave Thomas, who was an orphan and a high school dropout yet started Wendy's restaurants; the list goes on and on. We are what we think about. Think great thoughts and do great things.

⏱ Fly Like a Bumblebee

No fear, no doubt. This is it, look out! Success is an amazing adventure. It is the process of having a dream and then pursuing that dream with your whole heart. It is getting to the point where you believe it is impossible to fail. I had the opportunity to meet Mary Kay Ash, the founder and president of Mary Kay Cosmetics. Mary Kay Ash is a remarkable woman who had a dream that others called impossible. She refused to listen to the naysayers, and went on to build a business that is now one of the largest cosmetic companies in the world.

The symbol for her company is a bumblebee and it represents the ability to do the impossible. Why? Because scientists and animal experts have emphatically stated that it is impossible for the bumblebee to fly because it has small wings and a big body. But the bumblebee doesn't know that it is impossible for it to fly, so it flies anyway! Folks, the only one that ultimately keeps you from being great is you, and your limiting beliefs. Stop saying you can't and start saying, "It's impossible for me to fail." And you, too, will do unbelievable things.

⏰ Hannibal, Overcoming the Obstacles

Hannibal was a great African general and statesmen. He overcame great handicaps and accomplished the impassable because he thought he could. He realized that the only real limits in life are those we impose on ourselves. Hannibal was from the city of Carthage, whose arch enemies were the Romans. In 220 B.C. a war started between Rome and Carthage. Hannibal's troops were greatly outnumbered and had fewer weapons and supplies than the great Roman army. Hannibal did not let that keep him from believing that he could win and then acting on that belief. He came up with a daring plan to defeat the Romans. He knew that he could not win in a frontal attack, so he decided to do the impossible, to attack from the rear, over the Alps. But that was said to be impossible because the Alps were impassable. He developed a strategy where he would use great African elephants to go over the Alps. He gathered his troops and they went over the Alps, the mountains that were thought uncrossable, and they successfully conquered the Romans. He went on to become one of the greatest military strategists and leaders of all times. We still repeat one of his classic quotes: "Either find a way . . . or make a way!" I implore you to go after your dreams, even those that people say are impossible. If there is no way, make a way! If there is

no path, then make one and be a trailblazer. Whatever you think you can do, you will see it can come true.

The process of changing my thinking was not easy, but I realized I was not living up to my potential. There was more that I could do and it was up to me to do it. I had waited long enough for life to drop success in my lap and it had not happened. I had been living as though I had a thousand years to live. Every minute is precious and it is up to me to make the most of the time I have here. Some-one asked: "What would you regret if you were to die and had not accomplished or tried to accomplish that which you could have done?" I have gone with the flow and I didn't like where the flow was taking me. I was tired of being broke, busted, and disgusted; tired of being a prisoner of circumstances. I decided to make a change. I realized I had to act on life or life would continue to act on me!

⏰ Self-Development

How do you make yourself a better, more productive, more effective person? The key is self-development! Just as a bodybuilder goes to the gym to develop his body and to gain strength and power, the same is nec-essary for development of your mind and of your inner strength. You must develop yourself by working on yourself. I do not mean just on the outer self by exer-cising. That is important, but you must also develop your inner self and your mind. Do you develop your mind like your body, maybe by way of lifting books, tapes, and encyclopedias? No, the way is to read those books, listen to the tapes, and fill your mind with the information. Fill your mind with the pure, the power-ful, the positive, and program yourself for success. You can program your mind for success or let it be pro-grammed by others for failure. The key is making the decision to program yourself by reading and filling your mind with positive information. Create a new you. Give

yourself a makeover, not just for your face and hair but also for your mind and spirit. Just as you renew your body with food and cleanse your body with water on a daily basis, you should also renew your mind and cleanse your spirit on a daily basis. Read more positive books, think more positive thoughts, listen to positive music, and take time to pray and meditate on the good. Give yourself a daily dose of positive images and develop a new you, because the best way to build your wealth is to first build yourself!

The Key to Failure!

"I don't know the key to success, but I do know the key to failure! It is trying to please everybody!" This is a quote from Bill Cosby that expresses a real truth. In seeking success you must be an independent thinker. Some people are going to try to talk you out of your ideas and try to discourage you. An example is the story of the speaker who found one person in his audience who was unresponsive to his presentation and he concentrated all of his energies on that person, while ignoring the rest of the audience. At the end of the speech he still had not changed that person. Instead, he had alienated the rest of the audience by ignoring them! As you move to becoming an independent thinker, you must realize that everyone will not like your ideas, but you must believe in your dreams and know that you will either live your dreams or you will live someone else's dreams. Learn to think positive about your ideas and learn to like yourself enough that you can feel good when you please yourself. Do not let others discourage you and do not try to please everyone. If you love your ideas and move toward them with passion and enthusiasm, you will find many others who will love them also. Do not try to please everyone. Be an independent thinker!

⏰ Invest In Your Mind

Did you know that the average American reads one book a year while the average self-made millionaire reads one book a month? The average American looks at six hours per day of television while the average self-made millionaire looks at less than two hours of television. To change your thinking it is essential to change what goes into your mind. History proves that readers are leaders. The leaders usually have been the people who read more books. Readers are leaders. Benjamin Franklin once said, "If a man empties his purse into his head, no one can take it away from him. An investment in knowledge always pays the best interest." I implore you to go on a course of self-development. Read more books and listen to more positive and motivational tapes. You will then program your mind with the information that your success is possible and your mind will respond in due order.

⏰ Breaking the Mental Barriers

If you reprogram your mind to see that things are possible, then your mind will respond to the new information and go about making those dreams come true. First you must think it is possible; then you must believe it is possible; finally you must act! Case in point: for years it was said that it was humanly impossible to run the mile in less than four minutes. It couldn't be done. Then in 1954 a young man named Roger Bannister ignored the common belief and believed that it was possible. He prepared himself and eventually he ran the mile in 3 minutes 59 seconds. He broke the time barrier as well as the mental barrier. In 1964 a young high school runner named Jim Ryun ran it in less than four minutes, and now lots of people are able to run four-minute miles and the record continues to be broken. Why? Because people realize that it is possible; it can be done. They have a new mind-set and their mind is now able to go after what was thought to be impossible. If you think you can or think you can't . . . you are probably right! Reprogram your mind and go after your dreams and I know that you will start to break some barriers in your life. Have a great day!

⏰ Acres of Diamonds

The grass is always greener on the other side of the fence, it is said. Or could it be that they take more time and effort on their grass than you? I was talking to a friend who was disappointed because he didn't get a position that he thought was better than his present one, which is a position with great potential. I shared a true story with him about a farmer in Africa who became enthralled by the diamond trade. He was so anxious to get rich that he decided to sell his farm and go searching for the real riches. He sold the farm to the first person who came along and took whatever the man could give him and went to find riches. After many disappointing years without finding any diamonds, he finally gave up and threw himself over a cliff! Meanwhile, back at the farm, the man who bought it was walking across a stream one day and found a big shiny rock. He took it back and placed it on his mantel. A friend came one day from the city and saw the rock and was amazed. He said, "Wow! This is a diamond, probably one of the biggest diamonds I've ever seen! Where did you find it?" The man said, "I found it in the stream, but, hey, there are a whole lot of them around here. They're all over the place." The farm became known as "Acres of Diamonds." Friends, there are diamonds in your own backyard. You have diamonds all around you. In fact, there's a diamond inside of you! All you have to do is look! The grass can be just as green and even greener on your side of the fence. Feed and water your grass and it, too, will be beautiful!

⏱ Can We Change the World?
The Answer Is Yes!

Many people are concerned about the state of the world and are discouraged because they do not know that one person can make a major difference. One person can change the world. This thought, by an anonymous writer, shows that each of us can make a difference: "When I was young my imagination had no limits, I dreamed of changing the world. As I grew older and wiser, I discovered the world would not change, so I shortened my sights and decided to change only my country. But it seemed immovable. As I grew into my twilight years, in one last desperate attempt, I settled for changing my family, those closest to me. But alas, they would have none of it. And then as I laid on my deathbed, I realized if I had only changed myself first, then by example I might have changed my family! From their inspiration and enthusiasm then they could change the community, who could then change other communities, which would then change the country. If the country could be changed, then the world could be changed." The key to changing the world was to make the decision to first change ourselves!

How badly do you want it? Are you willing to do that which is uncomfortable in order to grow? Are you willing to undertake some difficulty and begin a course of self-development in order to stretch? Are you willing to go the extra mile in order to become a new you? Do you want it badly enough to go against the traditional way of thinking and develop a new mind-set so that not only do you think you can but you also believe, in your heart of hearts, that you can, and that you will? Think back and remember the story of the little choo-choo train that was moving up the hill against all odds, saying "I think I can, I think I can, in fact I know I can." You will soon realize that this little story is not only for children, but is for all of us. As we thinketh in our hearts, so as we are!

CHAPTER V

I've Got a
New Attitude!

In her song, "I've Got a New Attitude," Patti LaBelle sang about how she changed her look and changed her direction. It was an outward sign of an inward shift in her way of looking at the world; her perspective changed. Her way of thinking and acting changed. She had a new attitude! Sometimes it takes a new hat, coat, suit, or dress, but we must remember that real change comes from the inside out. The way you feel on the inside ultimately determines how you behave on the outside. You may feel good when you change your appearance, but to effect long-lasting change you must also change your inward appearance.

As we improve our state in life we know that we must dream Big Dreams and think Big Thoughts. We must consciously change our thinking to take on winner's thoughts. Then we must continue the quest and realize we must also get a new attitude, a new perspective, a new way of looking at the world, a new mind-set. Your attitude is a combination of your thinking, your emotions, your way of viewing events and circumstances around you, and your perspective. Your attitude is what you do and how you respond to the things that occur in your life.

Without question, attitude is a determining factor in our

83

success or failure. Attitude is a critical ingredient in the results that you will create in life. It is the key that starts your magnificent machinery and puts it into action. As Dr. Karl Meninger says, "Attitudes are much more important than facts," and he is right. Attitudes make the difference in success or failure!

⏰ It's All About Attitude

Your attitude is more important that the facts. Many times we face problems that seem insurmountable or we have circumstances in our lives that we cannot change. Well, our attitudes are much more important than the facts. The fact is that Stevie Wonder was born blind, but his attitude was, "So what? I am not going to let that keep me from being great." Spud Webb was born short, but his attitude was that he was not going to let his stature limit how far he was going to go. He won the dunk contest for the National Basketball Association. Helen Keller was born blind and deaf, in a time when they would cast those with disabilities into institutions, but she became one of the greatest women of all times. Friends, there are certain facts in your life that cannot be changed, but your attitude can overcome those facts. You can go on to do great things.

⏰ Attitude Is Everything!

Keith Harrell is one of my buddies from the National Speakers Association and a coauthor with me of the book entitled *Only the Best on Success*. Keith is a terrific speaker whose major topic is "Attitude Is Everything." There are billions of people in the world and one thing that everybody has is attitude. Some might have arms, legs, eyes, ears, and some may not, but everyone has attitude. The good news is that you do not have to buy it, it's free! But if you want an attitude that works for you, that improves your quality of life and enables you to accomplish your dreams, then you have to work for it, work on it, and work at it. It is not something you can sit around and wait for. To get a positive attitude you must make a decision. You must realize that you may not be able to control the things which happen *around you*, or the things which happen *to you*, but you can control the things that happen *"in you."* Attitude is everything! Make the decision to have a good, positive, and productive attitude, every day. Remember, it's up to you!

⏱ Another Great Day

It's another great day. I am excited about today like I am every day. Why? Because it's another great day! Now that sounds like a play on words, but in reality there are a number of things we have no control over, like the weather, but we can control our attitude to life. And we can have a great day, every day. A few weeks ago we had a major storm with fierce winds and heavy torrents of rain. I had a speaking engagement, and when I walked in someone said, "Have you ever seen anything like this rain? What do you think about this stuff?" I said, "It's a tough rain and a bad storm, but it's a great day." He said, "What, are you crazy?" I said, "No, I'm not crazy. When I woke up this morning, I looked outside and I saw the rain and the storm and I said, 'Wow! Another great day!' " He said, "What?" I said, "Yes, that's right! It's another great day! Why? Because when I woke up and saw the rain I was glad that I could 'see' the rain. Somebody made a whole list of things they were going to do today, places they were going to go, meetings they were planning to attend, and friends they were going to visit . . . and they didn't wake up! They cannot see the rain. I'm thankful every morning I wake up, because I've got another chance, another opportunity to slay some dragons and make a difference. And because I have that opportunity, it is a great day." Friends, every day is a great day if you get another shot at life. Les Brown says, "Every day you wake up without a chalk outline around your body is a great day!" Enjoy life! Live life to the fullest because "It Is Another Great Day!"

◔ Blessed and Highly Favored!

When you wake up every day, how do you greet others and how do you respond to their greetings? When people ask you how you're doing, do you say "Fine," "Pretty good," "Okay," "Not bad," "Just trying to make it," or "Life stinks?" Do you respond with gusto and enthusiasm, or just say what everybody else says, without any thought or feeling? How do you respond? Studies have shown that life responds to you as you respond to life. Zig Ziglar says "Outstanding! And getting better." Les Brown says, "Better than good and better than most!" My son, William, says, "Great!" And for years I said, "Terrific. I've never seen a better day . . . I woke up!" Then one day I met Zemira Jones, the president of WLS radio in Chicago, who, over the years, has become one of my best friends. When I first met him and asked him, "How are you today?" he responded, "I'm Blessed and Highly Favored." I asked him, "What was that? What did you say?" He said, "Blessed and Highly Favored." I said, "Wow! What a fantastic greeting. May I borrow it?" He said, "Please! And share it with lots of other people, because they need to know about the power of greeting and how they should speak positive and power affirmations into their lives." How you greet and meet others is a major part of how Life greets and meets you on a daily basis. Not only does it affect the people you speak to but, more importantly, it affects you. To say "I'm Blessed and Highly Favored" not only speaks about how you feel, but also your constant state of being. You are express-

ing how you feel now and how you're going to feel later.
You are expressing what is going on in your life and
what you want to occur in your life. You are calling
forth those things that be not, as though they were! You
are blessed and highly favored when you feel good and
when you do not feel good. You are blessed and highly
favored when you have money in your pocket and when
you are broke. You are blessed and highly favored
when things are going well and when there are challenges, because you are expressing your faith that
things are going to get better! Blessed and Highly Favored! It has become the motto of my staff, my family,
and my friends. I have shared it with so many audiences
that we have had to start a "Blessed and Highly Favored Club," which includes a newsletter and toll-free
daily positive message line. Greet and meet life with
excitement, enthusiasm and great expectations, and
life will respond in kind. Folks, it's "Another great
day" and "Yes! I am Blessed and Highly Favored!"

⏰ Expectancy

In order to be a success, you need to cultivate a positive
mental attitude. Every day you need to develop a positive outlook and a positive expectancy. A positive outlook is to look for the good in situations rather than the
bad. A positive outlook is to see the rain and be excited
because you know that plants need rain to grow, and
flowers need the rain to blossom, and without the rain
we would live in a desert. A positive expectancy is to
expect great things. There is an old saying that miracles
usually come to those who expect them and welcome
them. Expect great things and develop a positive mental attitude and you will be able to do great things. With
a positive mental attitude you can weather every storm
and know that with every blessing there is a burden and
with every burden there is a blessing. Aim for the blessings. Have a great day!

Most times when people speak of "attitude" they refer to a person's disposition, temperament or personality. We all know people who "have an attitude," which usually means a "bad attitude." A bad attitude refers not only to a poor disposition but also to a poor mental mind-set, a negative way of looking at the world. It is a way to see only the negative aspects of each situation . . . the glass is half empty rather than half full. It's a pessimistic view of the world. I once read that the definition of a pessimist is someone who complains about the noise when opportunity knocks!

Well, if there is such a thing as a "bad attitude," there must also be such a thing as a "good attitude," a positive perspective and an optimistic view! A positive mental attitude creates optimism and positive expectations versus a negative outlook and negative perspective. As my good friend Larry Winget says, "No matter what you do in life, you will do it much better with a positive mental attitude than a negative mental attitude."

⏱ Optimistic

As you develop a positive mental attitude, you will also develop optimism. Optimism is the attitude that expects good things to happen and the ability to believe that positive things are going to result from your actions. If you are optimistic, you develop a sense of expectancy to see the good in things rather than the bad. As you develop your positive mental attitude, remember to remain optimistic. Look for the rainbow and know you can't have a rainbow unless it rains! I like to use a phrase I heard: "I'm so optimistic that I am going fishing for Moby Dick in a rowboat and I'm taking the tartar sauce with me." Stay positive and remember that it is the positive thinker who most often sees the invisible, feels the intangible, and achieves the impossible!

Statistics show that attitude makes a difference, not only in achievement but also in physical health. People with a positive attitude tend to get sick less, and when they are sick, they get well quicker.

⏲ Live . . . Until You Die

Your attitude is much more important than the facts. While speaking to a senior citizens group, one lady stopped me and said that she was depressed because she didn't feel useful anymore. I asked her if she realized that Colonel Sanders didn't start Kentucky Fried Chicken until he was 65, Clara Peller didn't say "Where's the beef?" and become a popular TV star until she was in her eighties. And that George Burns won an Oscar in his eighties and signed a ten-year performance contract when he was in his nineties! Senior citizens are running marathons, opening businesses, scaling mountains, and doing all sorts of amazing things. They realize that they are all getting older, but their attitude is one of "I would rather wear out than rust out"! George Burns used to say his daily key to success was to get up and look in the obituaries; if his name was not listed, then he would get busy! He lived until he was a hundred years old and then he died. Not like many who retire from living at 65 and are simply buried years later. I implore you, do not stop living, until you die! As Satchel Paige, the great Negro League baseball player said, as he continued to pitch into his sixties, "Age is simply about mind over matter, if you don't mind . . . it don't matter!" Folks, enjoy life . . . all of your life!

⏲ Madam C. J. Walker

Madam C. J. Walker was a dynamic woman who did not let her initial circumstances keep her from achieving greatness. She was not a highly educated person, but a woman with a great positive mental attitude. Because of her attitude, she was able to rise above those who were more talented and more educated, and she was able to reach unbelievable heights and make millions of dollars. Madam C. J. Walker was the first black woman to become a millionaire in America. She realized that it is your attitude not your aptitude that ultimately determines your altitude! Develop a positive mental attitude and you, too, can rise to the top!

A friend shared a story about two little boys. One was an optimist and the other was a pessimist. A group of researchers conducted a study on positive and negative mental attitude and the boys were recruited for the study. First the researchers took the boy with the negative attitude and put him in a room full of the newest and most exciting toys and video games. There were all sorts of toys and games and machines that kids around the world had chosen as the absolute best. They left him alone in the room and said, "Have a good time." The second little boy, the optimist, was placed in a room that was quite different. He was placed in a room full of horse manure and he, too, was left there.

The researchers observed the two through two-way mirrors and were quite amazed at their findings. The pessimistic child just sat in the middle of the room and cried, while the optimistic child was laughing and smiling and jumping around, having a ball. When the researchers went into the room with the pessimistic child, they asked him why he was crying amid all the wonderful toys and games. He said that he was afraid to enjoy the toys because he was sure someone would take them away or they might break or that there would be something wrong with them. Then they went to the room where the optimistic child was still jumping around and having a ball, in the midst of the hip high horse manure. They asked him why he was having such a good time and he replied, "You can't fool me. With all this horse stuff I know there must be a pony here some-where!''

Friends, life is too short to halfway live your life. You should decide to live your life to the fullest and cherish every moment. Enjoy life. Isn't it a shame when people commit suicide and throw their lives away? Well, it is also a shame to throw your life away bit by bit and piece by piece by not living up to your potential. Whether you do it all at once or little by little, the end result is still the same: you don't live life to the fullest and therefore miss out on many of its real joys. ALWAYS, LIVE LIFE TO THE FULLEST!

⏱ The Uncommon Thought Creates the Uncommon Man

To be great it is necessary to think the uncommon thoughts, to do the uncommon things and to go after the uncommon goals. Rolo May, the great psychologist and author of *Man's Search for Himself*, said, "The opposite of courage is not cowardice but rather conformity." Conformity is people acting like everyone else without knowing where they are going and why. We dissolve into the mainstream rather than choosing to be distinct. We tend to go with the flow rather than directing the flow. President Theodore Roosevelt had a common philosophy, which made him stand out from the crowd. He said, "I choose not to be a common man. Me, it's my right to be uncommon if I can. I'll seek opportunity, not security. I do not wish to be a kept citizen humbled and dulled by having the state look after me. I want to take the calculated risk, to dream and to build, to fail and to succeed. I'll refuse to live from hand to mouth. I'll prefer the challenges of life to the guaranteed existence, the thrill of fulfillment to the stale calm of utopia. I will never cower before any master nor bend to any friend. It is my heritage to stand erect, proud and unafraid, to think and act for myself and face the world boldly and say, "This I have done." As Frank Sinatra said in one of his songs, "I Did It My Way!" Folks, I say to you, do it your way! Think uncommon thoughts, do uncommon things, and, as Henry David Thoreau said, "If one advances confidently in the direction of his dreams, and endeavors to live the life which he has imagined, he will meet with a success unexpected *in uncommon hours.*"

Find Your Life's Purpose

I want to share with you today a story that I got from Dennis Kimbro, the author of *Think and Grow Rich: A Black Choice*. Dennis told a story about Malcolm X that he heard from Percy Sutton, the former Manhattan Borough president. As a young lawyer, Percy Sutton represented Malcolm X in a court case and had won against overwhelming odds. It was a very intense court battle between Malcolm and his adversaries. As they were leaving the courthouse, Malcolm's supporters were on one side and his adversaries were on the other. Malcolm and Percy Sutton had to be protected by a number of bodyguards as they made their way to a long black limousine. Percy Sutton was so scared he could hardly speak, while Malcolm was as cool as a cucumber. Percy asked him, "Minister Malcolm, how can you be so cool in the face of all this danger, here where you could lose your life any minute?" Malcolm calmly replied, "I hadn't even noticed any danger. My mind is thinking about other things, things other than my mortality. But the reason I am not worried is because of a story I heard which gave me a new perspective on life. Brother Percy, years ago I was told a story about an old worker named Omar who had a dream and had seen the face of death. He woke up and ran to his Master and asked, could he have the fastest horse so he could escape death. The Master gave him the swiftest horse. Omar rode without stopping for three days. He did not stop for food or sleep or provisions. He rode as fast as he could. After three days the road branched into seven separate roads. He took the one to the far right but soon changed his mind. He took the one to the far left but changed again, and continued to vacillate from road to road until he had one left. He took that road and rode fast and strong. After he rode about 500 feet, the face of death appeared and said, 'Omar, Omar, why have you kept me waiting for three days?' " Malcolm X turned to Mr. Sutton and said, "The moral of this story is that you can run and you can hide, you can twist and you can turn, but no matter what you do, you can't get out of this life alive." So while you're here you'd better find your life's purpose, live life to the fullest, pursue excellence, and live your dream because you can't get out of this life alive!

⏱ What Drives You!

I was speaking at a school and a young woman came up after my speech and was very excited. She said she liked the speech and the information, but she wanted to know if it really worked. "Does this stuff really work?" She then asked me a question to help her to decide if it really works. She said, "Mr. Jolley, what kind of car do you drive?" It kind of took me by surprise and for a moment I was stunned because I do not equate the kind of car that one drives with one's level of success. I looked her in her eye and told her, "You know what, in all reality it doesn't really matter what I drive right now. The key is what drives me! If I am driven to live my purpose and driven to a life of excellence, then I will be able to purchase and drive whatever I want!" In life it not what you drive that counts, but it is what drives you! Pursue excellence and drive the best . . . YOU!

🕐 Excellence vs. Perfection

Webster defines *excellence* as "that which is superior of high quality, that exhibits first-class quality." *Perfection* is defined as, "the state of being perfect, without fault or defect" and that which states that anything less than perfect is unacceptable. Well, many say they are perfectionists and only want perfect results. They say that "practice makes perfect!" Yet in reality, "practice makes improvement." I do not strive for perfection but rather for excellence. I strive for constant and never-ending improvement and to constantly better my best! My goal is to be better today than I was yesterday and to be better tomorrow than I was today.

Hank Aaron had twice as many strike-outs as he had home runs, but he still hit more homers than anyone else! He was not perfect but he was excellent. I say that you should strive for excellence and not perfection because excellence allows you to constantly better your best. A. L. Williams said it best when he said, "All you can do is all you can do, and all you can do is enough. Just make sure that all you can do is absolutely all that you can do!" Martin Luther King, Jr. put it so wonderfully when he said, "If a man is called to be a street-sweeper, he should sweep streets even as Michelangelo painted or Beethoven composed music or Shakespeare wrote poetry. He should sweep streets so well that all the hosts of heaven and earth will pause and say, 'Here lived a great streetsweeper who did his job well.' " Strive for excellence, not perfection, and always try to better your best!

🕐 Excellence . . . the Little Extra!

When we talk about excellence, many people think it is so very difficult, so very demanding that it is not possible. And so they do not even try. Yet excellence is, by its definition, to do the little things, to go the extra mile, to try harder and give a little more on a daily basis. See, once you get the habit of giving your best, you will start to see the results. John Hess said, "A race horse that can run a mile a few seconds faster is worth twice as much because the little extra proves to be the big difference." There is a verse that states that the difference between ordinary and extraordinary is just a little "extra." And the difference between try and triumph is just the little "umph." The little extra can make a big difference. Give a little extra on a daily basis and you will realize that excellence really does pay the best dividends!

⏲ Hyacinth Morgan

Hyacinth Morgan is a woman I met while speaking at a college whose story inspired me. Hyacinth came to America at the age of twenty with a sixth-grade education. Her English was poor, but her desire to succeed was great. She started working as a housekeeper and began improving her English. After five years of working she saved enough money to go back and get her two children, whom she had left with her mother back on her small native island. When she returned to her country to get her kids, she had to pay back taxes, which depleted her savings. She worked another three years, saved, and brought her kids back to America. She began working again as a domestic, and did that for five years while working on her GED. She finally earned her diploma and enrolled in a local community college with the dream of becoming a doctor, but she was told that it was not possible because of her limited educational background. But again, her desire to succeed was great. She earned straight A's and was eager to go to a school with a Pre-Med program. But she was rejected by every school in the country because she was too old, now well past forty. But Hyacinth did not give up. She kept pushing until finally the people at Johns Hopkins University in Baltimore saw her grades and heard her story and accepted her into their Pre-Med program on a full scholarship. Friends, this is a true story of determination and inspiration that proves that if you can dream it, you can do it. A dream mixed with faith, confidence, determination, and persistence cannot be denied. Remember, all things are possible if you can just believe!

⏰ The Talking Bird

One of my favorite stories is about a rare talking bird that could speak five languages. A man heard about this rare talking bird and set out on a worldwide search for it. After an exhausting search he stopped in a pet store to ask for more information and it was there that he found the bird! He told the owner that he had to go on a short trip, but to please send the bird to his house in two days. When he arrived home in two days he asked his wife if the bird had arrived, and she replied, "Yes." He said, "Where is it?" And she said, "In the oven." "What? That was a one-of-a-kind bird that could speak five languages!" And his wife said, "Well, why didn't it speak up?" Most of us are like that bird. We have skills and talents that could change our lives, but we won't speak up and show the world what we've got to offer! Folks, let others know of your skills and talents. Let them know that you are unique. There is no one exactly like you. No one!

⏰ Speak Up

If you want something in life, you have to be willing to speak up and let people know what you want. We talked previously about the bird that would not speak up and therefore became someone's dinner. Well, the same is true for most people: they do not ask. The Bible says, "Ask and you shall receive." Well, the converse is also applicable: Don't ask, and you probably will not receive. Most people receive not because they ask not. As my friend Larry Winget of Win Seminars says, "If you want more out of life, you must ask more out of life!" Ask and you will receive, don't ask and you will only get what life throws your way and not what you want. If you want to g-e-t, then you need to a-s-k.

After you start to speak up, then you must also be concerned about the inner conversation that we all experience. Our inner conversation is the conversation that we either think or verbalize to ourselves. This inner conversation may seem harmless or inconsequential, but it is actually very important because it has great influence on our actions and our attitudes. Our attitude not only determines our actions but it also is connected to our inner conversation, which can also affect what we will and will not do. We must learn to control our inner conversation.

⏱ Now, Shut Up

Have you had days when you didn't want to get out of bed? Not because you're sleepy but because you are sick and tired of problems and would rather just stay in bed? Well, everybody has days like that. But the key to overcoming those days is to change your inner conversation, your inner communication. When that communication tells you that you don't have any reason to get up, you have to learn to respond by saying, shut up! That is right, just say shut up and then tell yourself to get up, get up and get going, get busy! Because nobody is going to do it for you but you. Depression is usually the result of negative inner conversation. Get up and listen to something positive (like the Motivational Minute) or read something positive (like *It Only Takes a Minute to Change Your Life*). Make a list of affirmations that you can recite on a daily basis. Say things like "Today is going to be a great day because I've decided that it will be. There are no two leaves alike, no two snowflakes alike, and no two fingerprints alike. No one was born to do what I was born to do.'' Wake up, get up, so you can go up! Make the decision to have a great day!

Reap and Sow

If you want more out of life, then you must put more into life. It sounds simple. The more you give, the more you get; the more you sell, the more money you make; the more seeds you sow, the more plants you reap. Most people are waiting for their ship to come in, but they haven't sent any ships out! They want the plants to grow but they haven't planted any seeds. Look, the farmer doesn't go out and sow ten seeds and expect a hundred plants. No, he plants lots of seeds and knows that some might not come up but the more he plants the more he gets. It's as old as time: as you sow, so shall you reap. That means you've got to get busy. You've got to make it happen! If you want more out of life, then you've got to put more into life. Believe and you can achieve!

The Creative Shoeshine Man

To be a success, you must find imaginative ways to overcome some of the obstacles that you will be presented with. You've got to be creative. Les Brown tells a story about a busy executive who was on his way to a meeting and was always rushing from one place to another. As he left his office he was approached by a shoeshine man who said, ''Hey, my man, you've got some crummy-looking shoes. Why don't you let me give you a shine?'' The businessman said, ''No . . . I don't have time'' and every block for the next six blocks he was approached about a shoeshine and gave the same answer, ''No . . . I don't have time for a shoeshine.'' Well, at the seventh block he walked past a shoeshine stand and the man was counting: "97, 98, 99, 100." He then said, "My friend, you look like a busy man so I apologize for the interruption. But today is my birthday and I made myself a promise that I would give a free shine to the one hundredth person who came by my stand and you are that person. Please allow me the opportunity to give you a shine and honor my promise." So the businessman sat down, and the shoe shiner went to work and worked diligently. He popped the cloth and worked so hard that perspiration soon fell from his brow. He gave the busy executive a terrific shine, in fact the shoes looked like they were brand-new. As the businessman was preparing to leave he said, "What is your regular fee?" The shoeshine man said, "Five dollars, sir." The businessman gave him a ten and said "Happy Birthday." The shoe shiner stood there for a few minutes and then said, "97, 98, 99 . . ." Friends, this story simply shows that we must be creative and use our wits, because many times that will be all that we have. Be creative!

Life makes no promises except that it will be challenging. It seems like it is part of the by-laws, that life is difficult. Yet I am confident it becomes infinitely more pleasurable and much more easy if you go about your day with a positive rather than a negative attitude.

In going after your dream, you must be creative, you must believe that you can achieve, and you must have a mind-set that will consistently tell you that "It is possible" and consistently say "Yes I can," "Yes I can," "Yes I can!" You need an "*I can*" attitude, a "*yes*" attitude, an attitude that makes a difference. Charles Swindoll said, "I am convinced that life is 10 percent what happens to me and 90 percent how I react to it." And so it is with you. We are in charge of our attitudes! Make the decision to make every day a great day. Make the decision to get . . . A NEW ATTITUDE!

CHAPTER VI

Just Gotta
Keep Kickin'—
Never Give Up!

If dreams are the seed for success, then what is the key to success? The answer is persistence and perseverance! You can never give up on your dream. In going after your dream you will have some challenges, some roadblocks, but you must persist. You've got to be creative and use all of your talents to overcome life's obstacles. We must look for the opportunities in life, and if there are no opportunities we must make some. We must take the lemons and icy-cold responses that people throw on our dreams and make them into lemonade! We've got to believe in ourselves and make a commitment to persist, to never give up! In other words, once we get an "I can" attitude we must then get an "I can" aptitude. We must make a commitment to take consistent and persistent action. *You just gotta keep kickin'!*

The Two Frogs

Once upon a time there were two frogs going down a country road. A great storm came up and they became confused. The wind was blowing so hard that they got separated and lost. In the confusion the first frog fell into a bottle of milk. He looked around, got angry,

cursed life and its bad breaks, and started crying and complaining about the problem and how bad life was. He whined and complained and focused his energies on the problem and he soon gave up and died. The second frog also fell into a bottle of milk, but he had a different attitude, a different perspective, a positive perspective. He didn't like the fact that he fell into the milk. He didn't like the tough breaks that life had thrown him, but he directed his energies to the solution rather than just the problem. He kept on hopping and kept on kicking; he didn't give up. He realized it is not so much what happens to you, but the key is what you do about it! So he started kicking and he kept kicking. He kicked and he kicked until he churned the milk into cream. He continued to kick. He kicked and kicked until he churned the cream into butter and eventually he walked out. Friends, life is not going to play fair. There will be times when life throws you some curve balls, and your ultimate success or failure will depend on whether you sit around angry at life, concentrating on the problem and how unfair it is, or whether you concentrate on the solution to the problem. I have found, without a doubt, that the key to success is not what happens to you but what you do about what happens to you.

Just Gotta Keep Kickin'
Lyrics by Willie Jolley

*In everybody's life you know some rain's gonna fall
At everybody's house sometimes trouble will call.
But when trouble stops by you can just sit there and
     cry,
Or you can make up your mind you will stand up and
     fight.*

*People listen closely to the sound of my voice,
Success in life is never due to chance but to choice.*

You choose to go on, to go through the storm,
Or you choose to give up and give in when things start
to go wrong.

It's up to you, whether you win or lose,
If you want to reach the top,
You must believe deep in your heart.
Give it your all, everything you've got,
And never, ever, ever, ever stop!

You've gotta keep kicking, keep on moving,
You gotta keep striving, keep on trying.

I know you can't control which way the wind's gonna
blow,
But you determine which way your boat's gonna go.
If the wind is blowing from the north,
but the south is your chosen course,
then you've got to use the flow,
to make it go where you want it to go.

The race in life does not go to the swift or the strong,
But to the one who just keeps moving along.
The one who claims the winner's cup, even when the
race gets rough,
Is the one who keeps kickin' and never gives up!

These are the lyrics to a song I wrote that speaks to the
fact that success is a matter of never giving up. It is a
statistical event. You've simply got to keep trying. You've
got to persist. After you develop a new attitude, a new
mind-set, a new determination, and a new way of looking
at the world, then there is still some more that you have to
do. You have a dream, you see the goal, you've got a new
attitude, you believe it is possible that you really can
achieve your goal, then you start out toward your goal and
the problems and the challenges start to appear. Doors are
closed in your face, people say ''No!'' to your ideas.

Mountains appear in your way. What do you do now? Do you give up? NO!

You must make a focussed decision to keep going. If you want success and you want to reach your goals, then you must decide to never, ever quit; you must decide to persist. Persistence, the process of never giving up, is the direct response of a positive mental attitude. It is the action step that is the key to all success stories.

One of my favorite stories of persistence is the story of W Mitchell. When I started my quest for self-development I would constantly hear the name of W Mitchell on tapes by Zig Ziglar and Anthony Robbins and many of the other great speakers of our time. I was intrigued with the inspiring story of persistence and determination about this man who refused to give up, even when the circumstances and obstacles in his life were overwhelming.

A few years ago I met Mitchell. He was as kind and warm to me as though we had known each other for years. We have since become good friends. I have heard him tell his story, as only he can tell it. It constantly reminds me that it really doesn't matter what happens to you in life, it only matters what you do about it.

⏱ W Mitchell, the Man Who Would Not Die!

W Mitchell is a man who exemplifies overcoming life's obstacles. He is respectfully called "the man who would not die" because he never gives up. Twenty years ago Mitchell was a student who worked part time as a cable operator in San Francisco. Between school and work, he found time to ride his new Harley-Davidson motorcycle for recreation. He lived for times when he could get out on his bike and feel the refreshing wind blow on his face. One day while taking a ride, he was crossing an intersection and suddenly saw a truck running a red light. The truck slammed into Mitchell. He was knocked to the ground and as he laid there in agony he smelled gas and realized that he was covered with it. Suddenly there was an explosion and the bike went up in flames, and then the fire spread and soon engulfed Mitchell in flames. He became a human torch and was completely burned from head to toe. He lost his fingers and toes and was left with no resemblance to his former self. He went through months and months of agonizing surgery and rehabilitation, but he never gave up. He finished his education and went on to start a business that soon became very successful. In fact, he was able to purchase a private plane that he piloted. His plane became his passion and he spent all of his spare time flying. One evening, while in flight, the plane started experiencing engine problems. He attempted to land but lost control and crashed. When he awoke after months in a coma, he found that now he was paralyzed from the waist down! He sat and looked at himself and saw a burned man who was now paralyzed and forced to live the rest of his life in a wheelchair. Others expected him to give up, but Mitchell refused to. He said, "There used to be ten thousand things that I could do; now there are nine thousand." He went on to share his story with others and has become one of the top motivational speakers in the world. He owns homes in Colorado, California, and Hawaii. He truly lives life to the fullest. He lives the life that he talks about. It's not what happens to you that counts. It's what you do about it.

⏱ Never Give Up!

So many have asked me what do you do when life throws you a curve ball, when Murphy's Law comes into play. Murphy's Law? You know, "Whatever can go wrong, will go wrong, at the worst possible time." I once heard someone say that in life you've either got a problem, just left a problem, or you're on your way to a problem. But even with Murphy, the key to your success is not to give up: just don't give up. This a portion of a very popular poem called "Don't Quit." The author is unknown but the meaning is so very clear.

When things go wrong as they sometimes will,
When the road you're trudging seems all uphill,
When the funds are low and the debts are high,
When you want to smile but you have to sigh,
When care is pressing you down a bit,
Rest if you must but don't you quit.
Life is queer with its twist and turns,
As every one of us sometimes learns,
And many a failure turns about,
When you might have won, if you'd stuck it out.
Don't give up, though the pace seems slow,
You might succeed with another blow.
Folks, don't quit no matter what.
Make up your mind that you are never going to give
*   up.*

⏰ Don't Quit!

Stuff happens! That is a part of life. As long as we are blessed to stay on this earth, we will have to pay a price of constantly dealing with the obstacles and challenges that life presents. But we can win, if we just persist. Never give up! This is "Don't Quit Part 2."

Often the goal is nearer than,
It seems to a faint and faltering man.
Often the struggler has given up,
When he might have captured the victor's cup.
And he learned too late when the night slipped down,
How close he was to the golden crown.
Success is failure turned inside out,
The silver tint of the clouds of doubt,
And you never can tell how close you are,

It might be near when it seems afar,
So stick to the fight when you're hardest hit,
It's when things seem worse that you mustn't quit.

There is an old saying that is states that "Winners never quit and quitters never win!" To be great you must be persistent and never, ever give up on your dreams, because one is not finished when he or she is defeated. One is only finished when one quits! Remember if you can dream it, you can do it. Have a great day!

I have found that the true definition of greatness is when you have ordinary people who do extraordinary things, people who persist and simply refuse to give up. Persistence compensates for every disadvantage and every limitation that would ordinarily keep people from going after their dreams. Persistence is the asset, the action step that turns your dreams into realities. Determination is an attitude, but persistence is an action, the action of never giving up!

⏲ Persistence

If you want your dreams to come true, then it is absolutely necessary that you be persistent. Of all the qualities that create winners, the most important is persistence. You have got to keep trying, keep trying, keep trying and resolve in your mind that you will never give up. Never! Persistence breaks down resistance. Life is going to say, No! People are going to say, No! But if you persist, then life will finally have to say, *Yes!* It's a law. Just like the law of gravity, which says that whatever you throw up will come down. The law of averages says that if you keep asking long enough, you are going to get a "Yes." It's got to happen! This is a quote from former president Calvin Coolidge: "Press on. Nothing can take the place of persistence. Talent will not; the world is full of unsuccessful people with talent. Genius will not; unrewarded genius is almost a proverb. Education alone will not; the world is full of educated derelicts. Persistence and determination alone are omnipotent." As I like to say in my seminars, "You've got to knock and knock and knock and knock and knock, until you knock it open or you knock it down!" In the confrontation between a stream and a rock, the stream always wins—not through sheer strength but rather through consistent persistence and perseverance!

⏱ The Fear of Failure

One of the biggest problems that keeps people from going after their dreams is a fear of failure. People are afraid of failure but do not realize that failure is a part of success. Every successful person has had some failure. But they use the failure, learn from the failure. They make failure their teacher, not their undertaker. In his quest to invent the light bulb Thomas Edison failed over 10,000 times, but he refused to give up. When asked why he did not give up, he said, "I didn't fail. I just discovered another way not to invent the lightbulb!" William Shakespeare said, "Our doubts are traitors, and make us lose the good we oft might win, by fearing to attempt." Don't be afraid to fail. In fact, look forward to failure, because if you fail and learn from your failure you are essentially closer to your goal. There is the story of a man who failed in business at the age of 21; was defeated in a legislative race at age 22; failed again in business at age 24; his sweetheart died when he was 26. He had a nervous breakdown at age 27; lost a Congressional race at age 34; lost another one at 36; lost a Senatorial race at age 45; failed in his effort to become Vice-President at age 47; lost a senatorial race at age 49; and at age 52 was elected President of the United States! His name was Abraham Lincoln! Folks, you can never give up! Don't let failure get you down. It's a part of success. Learn from your failures. Make failure your teacher, not your undertaker! Just remember people are not finished when they are defeated. They are only finished when they quit!

⏱ Importunity = Persistence

One of my favorite stories about persistence is from the eleventh chapter of the book of Luke, where Jesus shares this parable. "Suppose you went to a friend's house at midnight, wanting to borrow three loaves of bread. You would shout up to him, 'A friend of mine has just arrived for a visit and I have no food in the house. Could you loan me a loaf of bread?' He would call down from his bedroom, 'Please don't ask me to get up. The door is locked for the night, and we are all in bed. I can't help you at this time.' Though he wouldn't get up as a friend, if you keep knocking long enough he will get up and give you everything you want, just because of your importunity [persistence]."

Of all the qualities that ultimately make a difference in the quest for success, persistence is definitely the key to achieving your goals. Imagine that you were out last night and did not eat dinner because you were just too busy. When you finally got home, you were too tired to eat, so you just fell into bed. The next morning you wake up with severe hunger pains. Your stomach is growling and making all kinds of noises. You are simply starving. You go to the kitchen and open the refrigerator and it's wiped out, absolutely nothing is in there. You then go to the cabinet and open it up, and it's completely empty. Not even a cracker! Your stomach is growling, you're starving and you have no food. You've got to get something to eat. *What are you going to do*? Are you going to go to the store? to 7-Eleven? to McDonald's? to a friend's house? What are you going to do?

You run to the grocery store, but there's a sign on the

door that says, "There is a problem with the heating system and the store is temporarily closed." You run down the street to the fast-food store and when you get there the doors are locked. The sign says the employees are on strike and there are no replacements until later that day. You run frantically to another fast-food place and it's closed because their water pipes broke. You are starving! What are you going to do now? Are you going to go to a friend's house, to a restaurant, or to another grocery store? What are you going to do? What are you going to do?

Folks, I submit to you, that not one person, not one person said, "I'm gonna give up." You didn't even think it! Why? Because when you are hungry, when you are in dire need of food, then you will keep going until you are fed!

Well, the same is true for your success. You must keep going after your dreams. You must persist. You can never, ever give up! No matter how many doors are slammed in your face. No matter how many mountains and obstacles you encounter, you must develop a no-quit attitude. Never give up, never quit. Persist!

If you look closely at an ant you will see that it is an incredible creature because it never gives up. If you see an ant going along its way and you put a leaf, a stick, or a brick or anything else in its way, it will climb over it, go under it, go around it or do whatever is necessary to get to its goal. It never stops. It will never give up. It keeps trying, keeps moving, keeps going after its goal. In fact, the only time an ant stops trying is when it dies. Not only does an ant never give up, but it is always preparing for the winter. It prepares and thinks constantly about tomorrow, unlike the grasshopper, who only thinks about today. The grasshopper thinks summer all summer, while the ant thinks winter all summer. When the winter comes the ant is able to live with some comfort while the grasshopper suffers. The lesson is that the ant works diligently to prepare for the hard times that will come, because sooner or later . . . they will come.

We should all take a lesson from the ant. We should work diligently every day, and we should be committed to setting goals and going after them. We should plan for to-morrow. Then we should never give up, no matter what obstacles are thrown in our way. No matter what problems beset us or what circumstances we find ourselves in, we must never give up. We've got to keep going after our dreams and striving to reach our goals. We must always prepare for the future and think about the needs of winter while yet in the summer. We should plan and prepare for tomorrow. We should put something away for a rainy day. Because just as there is sunshine, there will be rain, and just as there is summer, there is going to be winter. Work hard, prepare for the difficult times and most of all . . . NEVER GIVE UP!

CHAPTER VII

What's Love Got To Do With It? . . . EVERYTHING!

Tina Turner asked the question, "What's love got to do with it?" But she did not give the answer. Many would ask, "What does love have to do with changing your life, what does love have to do with success?" The answer is . . . Everything! Love has everything to do with it, because love is the most powerful emotion on earth. Love has the capacity to heal and to cure, to build and to restore, to renew and reform, to translate and transform. Love hopes all things, bears all things, believes all things and endures all things. Love conquers all . . . and love never fails!

Margaret Walker wrote that love stretches your heart and makes you big inside. Duke Ellington said that love not only means I am with you but also that I am for you, all the way! And Martin Luther King, Jr., said: "Hatred and bitterness can never cure the disease of fear. Only love can do that. Hatred paralyzes life, love releases it. Hatred confuses life, love harmonizes it. Hatred darkens life, love illuminates it. I've decided to stick with love, for hate is too great a burden to bear!" For you see, love, like anything else that changes your life, is a decision. Love is a choice which creates options. Hate is also a choice, but it removes options.

In the book *The Greatest Secret in the World*, Og Mandino stated that the primary ingredient for long-term success is to start each day with love in your heart. Love the sunshine that warms the bones, yet love the rain that cleanses the spirit. Love the light that brightens the way, yet love the darkness that allows us to see the stars. Love others, even our enemies, so much that they have no options but to learn to love back because love tears down walls and builds bridges. Greet and treat all whom you meet with love, and realize how it affects them. Yet, more importantly see how it transforms *you*! Once you realize that you cannot control the time, you cannot control the weather . . . the only thing you can control is yourself. You can choose to love in spite of anyone or anything. Remember, love never fails!

⏱ Love: Moving Mountains

They said it couldn't be done! They said that it was impossible, but Mahatma Gandhi and Martin Luther King, Jr., were men who believed that it could be done and realized that love never fails. Mohandas Gandhi, a man who tapped into the awesome power of love and used it to move mountains and redirect history, was commonly called *Mahatma*, which meant "great soul." He used that great soul power to free India from British rule. He taught the Indian people that the guns and the violent tactics of the British could not defeat the awesome power of love. He developed a nonviolent, love-centered movement that captured the minds and souls of millions and inspired them to go against the odds and accomplish that which others said was impossible. He led a group of unarmed people to win a war of independence against the armed and stronger British, and he did it with love. In 1947 India won its complete freedom from Britain.

A few years later the same techniques were employed by a young minister named Martin Luther King, Jr. He

employed this awesome soul force called love and took Gandhi's philosophy and reengineered it for America. Many told him it would never work and that the only way to fight fire was with fire, but he maintained that love never fails. Time went on to prove that he was right! Martin Luther King, Jr., shared through his non-violent campaign that love is the most powerful force on the earth. All the guns and dogs and firehoses in the world cannot defeat a people empowered by the awesome force of love. Gandhi and King proved that nothing, "no-thing," can compare with the sheer power of love! Love never fails! Try love!

TRY LOVE!
by Willie Jolley and Gerald Patterson

If you've tried everything and everything has failed
There is a message in these words that I tell
You don't need those guns or need the wars
There's a solution that will build not destroy

Try Love! Love is the answer to it all
Try Love! Love is the answer to it all

You been everywhere, all around this old world
Putting your faith in people who don't really even
*   care*
Well, don't give up and don't give in
Put your faith in Jesus and your broken heart He'll
*   mend*

Try Love! Love is the answer to it all
Try Love! Love is the answer to it all

To effectively love you must first learn to love yourself. Before all else, it is critical to make a commitment to love yourself, because if you don't love yourself you will start to misuse and abuse *yourself*. Studies have proven that self-esteem is a critical ingredient to long-term success. If you do not love you, then you will not wait for anyone else to abuse you. You will do it yourself. Or you will consistently seek out those who are abusive or do not hold you in the esteemed position that you deserve. You will belittle yourself and devalue yourself and you will talk yourself out of being all that you truly can be. Before all else, you must learn to love yourself and learn to appreciate and feel good about yourself. Some call this process developing a positive self-image or developing self-esteem but in reality it is learning to love and treasure *you*.

⏰ Learn to Love Yourself

Statistics show that those who are achievers do not let anything or anyone make them feel bad about themselves. They learn to love and appreciate themselves, because they know that their accomplishments are directly affected by their self esteem. Dr. Carter G. Woodson said, "If you can determine the way a person thinks, then you will not have to worry about what they will do. You will not have to tell them to go to the back door. They will go without being told; and if there is no back door, they will have one cut for their own special benefit!" Friends, you make it a part of your daily routine to say to yourself, "I like myself, I love myself, there are no two leaves alike, no two snowflakes alike and no two fingerprints alike. No one was born to do what I was born to do. I am a unique person who God has created for a special purpose and I know that God does not make junk!" Make a commitment to yourself to love yourself!

You have to learn to love yourself and feel good about yourself because if you do not feel good about yourself you will let anything and anybody talk you out of your dreams and distract you from your purpose and your personal mission in life. George Benson sang a song called "The Greatest Love of All" which stated that the greatest love is inside of us. To love self is the greatest love of all. Yet so many never ever learn to love themselves. Have you ever noticed people who cannot stand being alone, not because of a fear of loneliness but rather because they do not like who they are alone with . . . themselves! You must learn to love yourself. Barbara DeAngelis wrote if you aren't good at loving yourself it will be difficult to love anyone else.

Now, many will ask how can you learn to love self. Well, how many have heard a song that you didn't like the first time you heard it? But you continued to hear it every day until you started to sing along and tap your foot. You "learned" to love it. You can learn to love anything. Some folks are married to people who they have had to learn to love! In all seriousness, the way that we learn to love ourselves is that we must make it a part of our daily routine to speak good stuff to ourselves, we must "sweet-talk" ourselves.

Statistics show that 80 percent of most people's conversation is negative and self-defeating. Their internal communication is limiting and self-defeating and most of their external communication is negative. We must learn to love ourselves. If not, we will do things that will sabotage or self-destruct our success. What does love have to do it? Everything!

When we think of love we typically think of love as the emotional concept of romance. But love is far more than that. Love is a vast concept that has many distinct types. We love our friends, but we do not love them the same way we love our mates. Love comes in different forms. There are three major types of love: Eros, Phileos, and Agape.

Eros love is the romantic type of love we usually talk about in love songs. This is what we think about when we usually talk about love. It is the love between a man and a woman. It is love that has passion and longing, craving and desire. Phileos is the love between friends and family members. Phileos love is love that is normally called brotherly love. In fact that is why Philadelphia is called the city of brotherly love. It was taken from the word phileos. Finally, there is Agape love, which is the love of God. Agape is the pure love that God has for us and that we have for God.

Eros Love!

Eros is the type of love that we are most familiar with, the romantic type of love. It is the love we hear about in songs about lovers. It is the love that people read about in romance novels. It is the love that moves a man and a woman to become one entity and to create other human beings.

This is a song that I wrote to express my love for my wife, it is called "Nobody But You." It shares how I love my wife so much "that I would crawl over broken glass to get to her!"

Nobody But You
Lyrics by Willie Jolley

*Have you ever been in a crowd yet you felt so all
      alone?*
Have you have been in a house that was not a home?
Have you ever been running fast but going nowhere?
*Thought you were in love but you knew you didn't
      care?*

That's how I was for so many years,
I was smiling on the outside
but on the inside there were tears.
Until the day, the day I met you,
That was the day all my dreams became true.

You, nobody but you,
Make me feel the way, the way that you do.
You, nobody but you,
I pledge all of my loving, all of my loving!

My friends all said that it was just a passing thing;
Infatuation, a simple little fling!
But they did not know that my life had changed,
And I would never, ever, ever be the same!

From the moment I saw you, something came over me,
I knew from the start that this was meant to be!
I took the vows and I'll gladly take the stand
Over & Over & Over Again!

Then they asked me how I feel about you.
I tell you just how I feel.
Every single day I fall on my knees and pray;
'Cause I'm so thankful for your loving,
Thankful for your loving!

You, nobody but you,
Make me feel the way, the way that you do!
You, nobody but you,
I pledge all of my loving, all of my loving!

Then they asked me how I feel about you.
I'll tell the world how I feel.
All the money on this earth,
Could not compare with what you're worth!
No amount of money, could ever keep me from loving
*   . . . YOU!*

No, No, Never, No, No!
Never Ever Ever, Never Ever,
Never Ever Stop Loving You!
Never Ever Ever, Never Ever,
Never Ever Stop Loving You!
I pledge all of my love to you!
Nobody But You!

No amount of money can compare with how you make
*   me feel.*
And I know this time, that it's for real.

So I'll do what I gotta do.
I'll climb over mountains.
I'll swim the deepest sea.
I'll go through hurricanes.
In fact, I'll climb over broken glass to get to you!
For You . . . Nobody But You!

⏰ The Magic Formula of Winning Relationships

Almost every day I am asked what is the secret to having a successful and enjoyable relationship. My wife and I not only live together but we also work together and play together. We are almost always together and many people marvel at how much we enjoy each other. What is the secret? The secret is to work on love on a daily basis.

I remember talking to a couple who had been married more than fifty years who gave me advice as I was preparing for my wedding day. They told me to remember that "love is more than an emotion, it is a decision! When you say I do! Then do!" Second, we talk about everything, not some things . . . but everything! When we have a problem, we talk about it immediately. And we work it out so that no one loses. We go for win/wins, where we both win! See, we learned that we don't have to argue, we can talk about it! We talk "to" each other and not "at" each other. If we talk to each other, then we are less likely to argue. It takes two people to argue! So if one doesn't participate, then you cannot have an argument! You have a choice. You can talk to each other, which is communication, or at each other, which leads to confrontation. If confrontation is not diffused by consideration, then that can lead to arguments, fussing and fighting, which is an altercation. Then somebody wants to win so badly that they won't let it die. Each side wants the last word, which leads to constant retaliation! Then things are said in a moment of heated conversation that make it impossible for reconciliation, which leads to breakup and noncommunication. Why go through all of that? Have a little patience and talk to each other. Learn to talk to each other and not at each other. Life will be much sweeter!

⏱ Who Loves Who More?

We talked earlier about how to communicate more effectively with our mates. Now let me share another secret that I have found to be most helpful. I make it a part of my daily routine to tell my wife I love her. And it's that simple. That is one of the secrets to our success. I have found there are days when I love her more than she loves me, and days when she loves me more than I love her. Because of this, we have a relationship where the power is constantly shifting. We have found that the person who loves the least in any relationship has more power than the one who loves the most! Therefore, the best relationships are the ones where the power is constantly shifting and vacillating from one person to another. Every day, whether I love her more or whether she loves me more, I make it a point to tell her I love her. Not only does it make her feel more secure but it also reminds me of my decision to be in love. Remember love is not just an emotion, it is a decision!

Phileos Love

The next type of love is Phileos, which is the love between friends. We all have friends and relatives we love and care about, yet it is a different feeling than when we fall in love. Phileos love is the love between friends that binds us together and moves us to share that which we have with others.

121

Call Me!
Lyrics by Willie Jolley and Bradley Thomas

Friendship is not about being convenient.
It's about being committed and consistent
Call me (you can call on me)—when you need me!
Call me (you can call on me)—pick up the phone and
        call me!

What good is a friend,
If you cannot depend on them?
When you're in need;
Said you need a friend;
Who'll be there thick and thin;
And you know will be a friend in deed.

You can call me, call me, call me, won't you call me!
If you need me, then call me!

Say you need a friend,
Who'll be there when you win.
But stand right by your side if you lose.
Someone you can call in the midnight hour;
And you know when you call, won't refuse.

Call me in the morning;
Call me late at night;
'Cause anytime you call me;
You know that it's alright!
I'm telling you once and I'll tell you twice;
For you I really care and I'm willing to share;
and I'm willing to sacrifice.

Call me; you can call me; oh yes!
If you need me; then don't delay;
Pick up the phone and call me right away!

Not gonna be a fair-weather friend,
I'm gonna be right here to the end!

A friend must be honest and true
Show their love, not by what they say but what they
     do!

For so, so long I used to think about love;
And showed my friends I loved them with kisses and
     hugs.
But then one day, Jesus passed my way;
Said no greater love can you give to a friend
Then if you would give your life for them!

Call me in the morning;
Call me late at night;
'Cause anytime you call me
You know that it's alright!
I'm telling you once and I'll tell you twice;
For you I really care and I'm willing to share;
And I'm willing to sacrifice.

Call me; you can call me; oh yes!
If you need me I'm standing near;
Just call my name and I'll be there;
Oh don't you wait and don't delay;
Just pick up the phone and call me right away!
My brother, my sister
You can call on me, you can call on me!

All love that is pure and magical moves beyond the physical to the spiritual. Have you ever had the experience that someone you knew needed help or needed you and at that moment the phone rings and it is that person! Isn't it interesting? Well, love that is sincere and committed always moves beyond the physical and moves past the emotional and moves to the spiritual.

Agape!

Agape is the love that is shared between the Creator and the creations. It is the love between God and his children.

It is a divine love affair between us and God. Agape love is really true love!

A friend asked me to sing at his wedding a special love song he wrote that expressed how he had constantly been in search of true love. His search always ended up in disappointment. But one day he found true love, which surprisingly had been within his grasp the whole time! I sang the song at his wedding and saw how so many were touched by the lyrics. It was not only inspiring for the audience but it was also inspirational for me. I have been sharing the song with people around the country and I want to share it with you. *True Love!*

True Love!
Lyrics by Danny McCrimmon

Our hearts have been confused so much;
With words and even with a simple touch.
We're blind to what is real;
Temptations make us yield.
Leaving us trapped in our own desires.

When faced with finding that true friend;
Sometimes we just don't know where to begin.
We're reaching out in vain;
Trying to place the blame.
When the fault lies within ourselves.

I thought I'd found that special love;
The kind that some people can only dream of.
But it was at the cross that I began to see the light;
TRUE LOVE Came In A Sacrifice!

No greater love can you receive;
Than this, if you would only just believe!
There's enough for everyone and it'll leave no heart
*   undone;*

'Twas grace that made it possible!
I've finally found that special love;
The kind that some people can only dream of.
'Cause it was at the cross that I began to see the
        light;
TRUE LOVE Came In A Sacrifice!

Oh, TRUE LOVE Came In A Sacrifice!
TRUE LOVE I Found My Paradise!
TRUE LOVE Came In A Sacrifice!
TRUE LOVE, The ONE Who Gave His Life!
And it was at the cross that I began to see the light;
TRUE LOVE Came In A Sacrifice!

True love is recognizing that love is a gift, which becomes perfect when it is unconditionally given and unconditionally received. It is the faith, the assurance, the confidence, the belief that we are loved and that love was given freely and continues to be given freely. Yet the acceptance depends on us. Whether we accept the love or reject it, it all depends on faith. Finally, it is important to state that love, all love, is more than an emotion. Love it is a choice. Love is a decision!

Do It Anyway

People are unreasonable, illogical and self-centered
Love them anyway!
If you do good, some people will accuse you of
        selfish, ulterior motives;
Do good anyway!
If you are successful, you will win false friends and
        true enemies;
Succeed anyway!
The good you do today will be forgotten tomorrow;
Do good anyway!
Honesty and frankness make you vulnerable;
Be honest and frank anyway!

125

*The biggest people with the biggest ideas can be
    shot down by the smallest people with the
    smallest minds;*
Think big anyway!
People favor underdogs but follow only top dogs;
Fight for the underdog anyway!
*What you spend years building may be destroyed
    overnight;*
Build it anyway!
*People really need help, but might attack you if
    you help them;*
Help people anyway!
*Give the world the best you've got and you'll
    sometimes get kicked in the teeth;*
Give the best you've got anyway!
*Do good and love and people will laugh at you
    and call you names;*
*Do good and love anyway . . . because Love never
    fails!*

AUTHOR UNKNOWN

⏱ A Winner's Attitude

**We talked earlier about CDI (Can Do It) and having a
winner's attitude. This means you truly believe you can
do it; and you truly believe you are going to win! You
can share love too, not only with people you know but
also with those who you do not know. The Golden Rule
states, "Do unto others as you would have them do unto
you." John Wesley said it so aptly:**

Do all the good you can,
By all the means you can,
In all the ways you can,
At all the times you can,

To all the people you can,
As long as ever you can . . .

Yes, you can! Even though others might laugh and be-little you. You can do amazing things if you just try love. CDI! Try love!

⏰ Love Is a Risk!

To give up, is to give in.
To give in is to give out.
To give out is to stop trying.
To Stop Trying Is To Do Nothing!
And We All Know That Where Nothing Is Ventured,
Nothing Is Gained, And Evil Flourishes
Where Good People Do Nothing.
Sometimes You Must Take A Risk!
It Might Be Challenging And Might Be Difficult,
But The Rewards Are Worth The Risk!

To Laugh Is To Risk Appearing The Fool.
To Weep Is To Risk Appearing Sentimental.
To Reach Out For Another Is To Risk Involvement.
To Expose Your Feelings Is To Risk Exposing Your
    True Self.
To Place Your Ideas And Your Dreams Before A
    Crowd
Is To Risk Their Loss.
To Love Is To Risk Not Being Loved In Return!
To Live Is To Risk Dying.
To Hope Is To Risk Despair.
To Try Is To Risk Failure.
But Risk Must Be Taken Because
The Greatest Hazard In Life Is To Risk Nothing!
The Person Who Risks Nothing, Does Nothing, And
    Has Nothing!

They May Avoid Suffering And Sorrow
But They Cannot Learn, They Cannot Feel.
They Cannot Grow, They Cannot Love.
They Really Cannot Live!
A Person Who Risks Is Truly Free!

AUTHOR UNKNOWN

🕐 Love Never Fails!

Love is patient and kind
Love is not jealous or boastful
It is not arrogant or rude
Love does not insist on its own way
It is not irritable or resentful
It does not rejoice at wrong, but rejoices in the right
Love bears all things, believes all things
Hopes all things, endures all things, Love Never
Fails!

(TAKEN FROM THE LOVE CHAPTER—
1 CORINTHIANS 13)

The Question Is . . . What's Love Got to Do With It?
The Answer Is Everything!

🕐 I Can Only Leave Love!

When I die . . . give all that's left of me away,
to children and old people that wait to die.
And if you need to cry, cry for your brother
who is walking the street beside you.
And when you think of me, put your arms around
*   anyone*
and give them what you meant to give me.
I will leave you something . . .

Something better than words or sounds.
Love doesn't die, people do.
So when all that is left of me is love
Give me away! I'll see you at home in heaven!

ANONYMOUS

CHAPTER VIII

Blessed Assurance!

"Now Faith is the substance of things hoped for, the evidence (the assurance) of things not seen!"

HEBREWS 11:1

Faith! What does it have to do with success? Well, in interviews with successful people around this country, about their secrets of success, almost all of them said the same thing. You must have faith in yourself, faith in your dreams and most importantly, faith in God!

The African culture calls it Imani; the Jewish culture calls it Emunah; the Muslims call it Imam. Whatever name you use, it still means the same thing—Faith! Webster defines *faith* as "complete confidence and assurance; firm belief and strong conviction, belief without doubt . . . in the loyalty and love of God!" Faith is the assurance, the blessed assurance, that God Is and that we believe that He Is! And we trust in that belief! Some would say that faith is belief without proof, but I agree with Elton Trueblood, who stated, "Faith is not so much belief without proof, but rather trust without reservations!"

Faith is the belief in someone greater than yourself; and then the action of stepping out on that belief. It is taking a thought and seeing it transformed into a belief. That belief

131

is then transformed to a concrete understanding, a knowledge. That knowledge continues to grow and continues to be transformed until the time that you know, that you know; and your know even knows!

Faith is the understanding that there is a Creator who empowers, enlightens, encourages, and sustains us, in the sunshine or through the storm. And faith, like everything else . . . is a decision!

Faith is a concept that many people do not understand and therefore do not take advantage of. We all have faith. . . . The key is what do we have faith in. Every day we exhibit faith. We walk into a room and when asked to have a seat, we do not check the chair to see of it is sturdy or if it will hold us. We simply sit down. We sit down without knowing whether it will hold our weight. That is called faith. Or we go get a job and the boss says I will pay you "this" amount of money to work here. Start tomorrow and I will pay you in two weeks. We work those two weeks without really knowing whether the boss can or cannot pay us. Then we are usually given a check that we start spending before we find out if it is good or not! Friends, that is a type of faith. Faith is a belief in, or an assurance of, that which we cannot actually grasp in our hands, yet that which we trust in. That is faith in the natural, which is a small part of the greater faith, that is spiritual. Yet faith is always a decision!

⏱ Faith Is . . .

Faith is the substance of things hoped for, the evidence of things not seen. The substance of things hoped for means the essence of things that you dream and desire, and the evidence, the assurance, the confidence, the proof of things not seen. In other words, faith is trusting in things that you cannot see, yet that you can see the results of. Many people doubt the existence of faith because they cannot see it. Yet they do not question the

existence of electricity, which they cannot see coming into their homes, but they see the results when they turn on a light! They cannot see the wind but they can see the results of a hurricane. They cannot see the radio and television waves, but they can see the results when they turn on the television and the radio. Faith is the substance of things hoped for and the evidence, the proof, of things not seen. Have faith!

Ten-thousand-dollar Faith

When we look at motivation we must realize that it is very different from inspiration. Motivation deals with the head while inspiration comes from the heart. Inspiration ignores logic and ignores the circumstances. It relies on faith. If you haven't got faith, you need to get it! If you have faith, then you should work to develop your faith, strengthen your faith, and help it to grow stronger. Develop mountain moving faith. Often we try to get ten-thousand-dollar results on ten-cent faith. It you want great results, you must have great dreams and great faith—great faith in God and a confidence that no matter what life throws at you, He will never leave you or forsake you. Then you've got to believe in yourself! You got to have the faith to believe that if you can dream it, you can do it. Because if you don't believe in you, don't expect others to believe in you! If you want something in life, then you've got to see it, think it, dream it, believe it, and go for it! And to make it a reality you've got to have faith. Remember that all things are possible if you can just believe!

Don't Faint

We all experience times when our faith is tested by the challenges of life. There are times when we have nothing else to hold on to except our faith. I was talking to a friend who called because she was going through a medical challenge. She had to have surgery and it was to be a serious operation. A few days after finding out about her condition, she was hit with another blow. Her ten-year-old son was diagnosed with a life-threatening disease that would leave him with a permanent heart condition! Her thoughts and fears for herself soon dissipated and she was only concerned with him. She called and asked, "Why me?" I shared with her that life is not fair and it is by its nature difficult. And it is most difficult when the problem is something you cannot control, no matter how much money, influence, or power you have. Those are the times you need faith. And you must be committed to that faith. I like to use the analogy that faith is like getting into a boat and making a commitment to stay in the boat, no matter what. If the boat hits rough waters, you must stay in the boat. If the boat starts to rock, you must stay in the boat. If the boat turns over, stay in the boat, even if it sinks . . . stay in the boat! Why? Because you will see that even though the boat has taken on water, you will be sustained in the midst of the storm. Scriptures state that, "They that wait on the Lord, shall renew their strength. They shall mount on wings as eagles, they shall run and not be weary, they shall walk and not faint!" Friends, life has rough moments and storms will rise, but if you can wait, and have faith, you will be sustained.

⏱ All Things Work Together for Good . . .

Once upon a time there was a wise Chinese father in a small community. This wise father was held in high esteem, not so much because of his wisdom but because of his two possessions: a strong son and a horse. One day the horse broke through the fence and ran away. All the neighbors came around and said, "What bad luck!" and the wise father replied, "Why do you call it bad luck?" A few days later the horse came back, with ten other horses, and all the neighbors said, "What good luck!" and the wise father responded, "Why do you call it good luck?" A few days later his strong son went out to the corral to break one of the new horses, and he was thrown and broke his hip. All the neighbors came over and said, "What bad luck!" and the wise father responded, "Why do you call it bad luck?" About a week later the evil warlord came through the town and gathered all of the strong, able-bodied young men and took them off to war. The only one he did not take was the boy with the broken hip. All the young men were killed in battle, and when the news reached the community, the neighbors rushed to the father and said, "What good luck!" and the father said "Luck? No! It is not luck! All things work together for the good, for them who love the Lord!" There may be times when things really look tough and when things do not go as you planned, but if you look hard enough and have faith, you will see that with every blessing there is a burden, and with every burden there is blessing. Every dark cloud has a silver lining, if you are willing to look for it and learn from it.

After you have set your goals, you've dreamed big dreams, you've done everything all the self-help books advised you to do, then life throws you a curve ball! Something happens that is not in the plans and it is something you have no control over. Some people call it "Murphy's Law" and others see it just as a part of life. In the book *The Road Less Traveled*, the first line really hits it on the head: "Life is difficult!" Life does not play fair, and sometimes life doesn't seem to care. It will throw things at you that will disrupt and distract, that will throw you off-track. When you have done all you can think of and are faced with situations that you cannot explain, contain, or control, then what do you do? YOU HOLD ON AND ACTIVATE YOUR FAITH!

⏰ It Came To Pass!

Les Brown talks about the fact that life will hit you on the blind side and at times will knock you down. But you must have the faith to endure the blow and to know that the future does not equal the past. There are greater things out there for you and you must have the faith to overcome the challenging times. Finally, he says, "If you get knocked down then you should try to fall on your back, because if you can look up you can get up!" Dr. John A. Cherry, another of my mentors, is the pastor of the Full Gospel AME Zion Church in Temple Hills, Maryland, which is one the largest churches in America and is the second largest Methodist church in the world. Building and pastoring such a large congregation has many challenges and his sermons share how it is necessary to understand that the Bible gives many secrets and clues for success if we would only seek it with diligence. He speaks about the fact that as you go forth in life and pursue that which God has given to you to do, there will be problems and challenges. And you will need faith, great faith, to meet those challenges. Throughout the Bible we see the phrase "it came to pass." Most people think this just means that something has occurred or is about to happen. It does mean that things will occur, things will happen, but that's not all. See, when things happen in life that are challenging and difficult, we must have the faith to understand the rest of the story; that when it "came to pass," it will pass, it does not come to stay.

In everybody's life there will be challenges that will test your faith, that will test your resolve. Yet while challenges do come, they do not come to stay, they must pass. If we can have the faith to simply believe, then we will see that we will grow because of those situations and that growth is what will separate the winners from

the "wannabes." We all have challenges. We all have difficulties; just remember that they "came to pass," they did not come to stay! Have Faith and Hold On, because it simply came . . . to pass!

Those are the times you need to muster up the inner strength that will help you to overcome those obstacles, the inner strength that is a direct result of your faith. It is the faith in God that sustains and holds you when all else has let you down, when all else is insufficient. It is the faith that gives you the assurance that through it all not only will you survive but you will thrive. I'm not talking about a faith that is just a placebo, one that simply pacifies you. I am talking about the deep faith that gives you the will to fight, the faith that gives you the guts to go on, the faith that inspires you to rise above your circumstances and to go on, in spite of the difficulties.

Like everything else in life, faith is a decision. And like all decisions, it only takes a minute to make that decision; it only takes a minute to change your life! The Bible shares a story about two thieves who are on the cross. They looked across to the great teacher from Nazareth, named Jesus, who was being crucified for teaching a new message to the people of Israel. One shouts out, "So you say that you're the Messiah. Well, since you're the Messiah, why don't you come down from that cross and save yourself, and us too while you're at it?" But the other thief says, "Why don't you be quiet, you fool! Don't you realize who you're talking to?" Then he turns to Jesus, the Christ, and says, "Jesus, please remember me when you come into your kingdom." And Jesus replies, "Today you will be with me in paradise, this is my solemn promise." (Luke 23:39–43) *The Living Bible*

This is a defining moment, because in just a minute a thief made a life-changing request. In that minute his life was changed for eternity. It only took a minute to change his life because he believed that there was a force greater than himself which could change his life. Because of his faith, he opened his mouth and asked a question that changed his life.

⏱ A-S-K

In order to make your dreams come true, many times you will need assistance. You will need help from someone else. Many times the person who can help is not far away, in fact is within your grasp. But many never ask for that assistance. They have such fear of rejection and so much mistaken pride, they refuse to ask for help. There are numerous people who are ready and willing to give help, but no one asks them! It's like the high school beauty queen who almost went to the prom alone because she didn't have a date. Finally, the class bookworm asked and she went to the prom with him. The other guys were afraid to ask because they assumed she had many requests and would reject their invitations. The little bookworm felt he had absolutely nothing to lose, so he asked. He asked and she said yes because no else had asked. He became the big man on campus, not only because he escorted the beauty queen, but because he had the guts to ask. Eventually he became her regular date and then her husband! If you want something out of life, you must be willing to A-S-K. Have faith, believe in yourself, and then be willing to act on that belief. Ask and you shall receive! Seek and you shall find! If you want to G-E-T, then you must A-S-K! And remember that all things are possible if you can just believe!

Matthew 7:7 says "ASK and it shall be given you, SEEK and you shall find, KNOCK and it shall be opened unto you. For everyone that asks receives and he that seeks finds and to him that knocks it shall be opened." As you believe, so shall it be done unto you! If you will take a second and look closely at these scriptures you will always find an action command that relates to the benefit you will receive.

Ask, and you shall receive; to ask means that you know what you want and are willing to ask for it and communicate your desire for it. Seek, and you shall find; to seek means that you are willing to take action, to look for it and search for it. Finally, knock, and the door will be opened unto you; knock means that you are willing to knock and keep knocking, to persist and persevere.

In each of these statements there is an action command, something we have to do in order for the second part of the statement to become a reality. We must take some action, display some faith, some belief that it is possible, in order to experience the fullness and rich blessings that we are capable of receiving.

"Ask and you will receive. Seek and you shall find. Knock and the door will be opened unto you." Conversely, if you do not ask, you probably will not receive; if you do not seek, you probably will not find; if you do not knock, the door will probably not be opened unto you. If you want something in life, then you, and I do mean *you*, must take some *action* if you want some *results*. This scripture shows that even with faith we must take some personal responsibility and take some personal action in order to have our faith released and activated. Wally Amos, the cookie king, says that you must have faith, focus, and follow-through. He says that God is not a one-idea God and therefore we can have the faith to believe in the dreams that we are given, focus to pinpoint our energies on the dream, and follow through to take the necessary action steps that will make the dream into a reality. A friend told me, "Faith is not only a fact, but it is also an act!" For faith to be effective you must take action because "Faith without works is dead!" Take action on your faith; reach for it!

Reach For It!
Lyrics by Danny McCrimmon

If You Need A Spiritual Blessing, You Should Come
   Expecting,
As You Reach, Reach For It, To Receive It By Faith.

*If Your Soul Needs Reviving, You'll Gain Strength In Your
        Striving,
As You Reach Reach For It, To Receive It By Faith.
Oh Reach For It, Just Reach For It,
The Lord Has A Blessing In Store For You.
All You've Got To Do Is Reach For It,
As He Reaches Out His Hand To Give It To You.*

We have all heard the statement "God helps those who help themselves." This is often mistaken for scripture but in reality it was a statement made by Benjamin Franklin! Although it is not from the Bible, it does have biblical significance. If you have the faith to believe, then you can release the power of God to take action in your life. It is like the other old saying, which also is not in the Bible but has significance to faith, "If you take one step, God will take two." We must have faith and act on that faith to receive the full measure we are capable of receiving. Faith is a fact and also an act! Act on your faith!

⏱ Work Hard, Work Smart, Trust God

We've talked about hard work, the need to be diligent and committed to our goals and not to rely on luck, which is by definition when opportunity meets preparation. Success comes from hard work. But it is also very important to work smart, to think about what you're doing, to plan, and be organized so you can maximize the benefits that come from your efforts. Remember that the most important ingredient is to trust God. Even when you feel you're prepared and ready for success, life will try to throw you some curves, knock you down, disrupt, distract, throw you off track. But just keep in mind that if God is for you, He's greater than the whole world against you! With faith, deep-rooted faith, it becomes impossible to fail. As one philosopher said, "PRAY, like it all depends on God,

and WORK, like it all depends on you!" Work Hard, Work Smart, and Trust God!

⏱ Hard Work Works

I received a call from a friend who said she liked the Magnificent Motivational Minute and wanted to share a saying she got from her mother that helped her reach her goals. That message is "Hard work works." There is no substitute for hard work. Hard work is to success what wet is to water, hot is to fire: they are inextricably connected. Success is not the result of luck or good fortune, but rather hard work. Someone once said, "I am a great believer in luck; the harder I work the more I have of it." In Proverbs it says, "Hard work brings prosperity, playing around brings poverty." William Penn wrote, "No pain, no palm; No throne, No throne; No gall, No glory; No cross, No crown!" Work hard and, remember, all things are possible if you can just believe!

Personal-enrichment faith is not a new concept, but for years very few realized that it could be connected to success. Most limited the concept of faith only to spiritual enrichment. It was not thought of as a way to run a business or as a success system. Faith was not thought of as a way to go beyond simply striving and surviving, to actually thriving. In this century a new way of thinking emerged that saw faith as a way not only to increase your spiritual wealth and prosperity but also your physical wealth and prosperity. It was made popular through the work of ministers like Dr. Norman Vincent Peale and then expanded upon by people like Dr. Robert Schuller. The prosperity concept of faith was further expanded by ministers like Kenneth Copeland and Dr. Frederick K. C. Price.

In *The Power of Positive Thinking*, Dr. Norman Vincent Peale showed us that through the use of a positive mental attitude, a proper state of mind, induced by simple prayer, one could produce spiritual and material success on earth. Dr. Peale stressed a simple yet meaningful message that was not a "pie in the sky" ideology but a theology which focused on achievement and accomplishment through prayer and real, deep-rooted faith.

⏰ Dreamers from the Bible

What kind of dream should you dream? How big should it be? Well, your dream should be bigger than you, something that dominates and consumes you. If you look through the Bible you see that those who accepted their dreams are those who were able to do the impossible. Jacob, Joseph, Daniel, and John are a few examples of those with whom God shared dreams and who were willing to let those dreams drive them to success. Joel 3:28 says, "I will pour out my spirit upon all flesh, and your daughters shall prophesy, your old men shall dream dreams and your young men shall see visions." Dare to dream and dare to succeed.

If you want great results and accomplishments, it is necessary to have great faith. Life by its nature is difficult. There will be times when your faith is the only thing that will sustain you. It will be the only thing that can keep you from going off the deep end. Even though it is difficult, if you have faith and a big dream, life can become the most wonderful and fantastic adventure you could ever experience. But it's all up to you. A big dream mixed with confidence, determination, persistence, and massive faith can make life the most wonderful adventure you've ever experienced. But you must use all the ingredients and you must believe that it is possible.

⏰ Don't Be Intimidated by the Obstacles

Once you set your goal and start on your way to achieve it, you will surely encounter difficulty. There will be some obstacles, but you can't allow them to intimidate you. When Moses brought the Hebrew children out of Egypt, he sent twelve spies to check out the land. Ten came back saying the land flowed with milk and honey but also had giants. Those ten spies wanted to give up because they felt that they were grasshoppers next to the giants. Only two put their faith in God. They were not intimidated by the giants because they had greater faith in God. They were willing to trust God and say that they could possess the land. Don't be intimidated by the obstacles. When God is for you, He's greater than the whole world against you.

One of my favorite Bible scriptures is taken from Deuteronomy, Chapter 30, where it is written, "I call heaven and earth to witness against you that today I have set before you life and death, blessings or curses. Oh that you would choose life, that you and your children might live!" We must choose to be happy, choose to be healthy, choose to be secure, and choose to be wealthy. Why do I say choose? Because success is a choice, not a chance.

⏰ Count Your Blessings

In life you are going to have problems! Someone once said that in life you've either got a problem, just left a problem, or you're on your way to a problem. But you must decide whether you will concentrate on your problems or whether you will focus on your blessings. I suggest that you make a commitment to count your blessings and not your problems. Unfortunately, most people count their problems and ignore their blessings, which always outweigh the problems. How can I be so confident of that? Because you are reading this book right now, which means you are still alive and able to read. I guarantee you that there are millions of people in graves who would give anything, anything, to be in your shoes right now, with whatever problems you have. Because if you are alive, you are blessed! And you have the ability to read, to see, to hear, or to communicate ideas. You might not have a lot of money or a lot of material things, but you are alive and therefore you are still capable of making some decisions that can make things better in the future than they have been in the past. As long as you are alive you have a shot! Count your blessings not your problems. A friend sent me a note that said, "When you are down to nothing, then God is up to something! Remember, when it's over your head, it's still under God's feet!" Count your blessings!

After having faith in God, we must extend our faith to a solid belief in ourselves. You must believe that it is possible to achieve not only what others call improbable, but also what others see as impossible. You must have a belief in self that makes you confident, without being arrogant, in the midst of the storm. Faith is the belief in what is unseen at the moment but which is possible for the future.

Not only are there different names for faith but there are also different levels or sizes of faith. There are people who have small faith and people who have great faith. You can have mosquito faith and mosquito dreams or elephant faith and elephant dreams. A mosquito can create and gestate a baby mosquito in a few days, while an elephant takes twenty-three months to create a new baby elephant. What kind of faith and dreams do you want? Small overnight mosquito dreams or BIG, MASSIVE ELEPHANT-SIZED DREAMS?

Throughout the Bible there are numerous examples of people who used their faith to release the power of God in their lives. They experienced miracles and supernatural evidences of the power of God, simply by taking action on their faith. Those miracles didn't just happen to the people in the Bible but have continued to happen throughout the years and are still happening today!

⏲ Maggie Johnson

I was recently traveling to a speaking engagement in Texas when I had the opportunity to meet a charming young woman named Maggie Johnson. Maggie just happened to be seated next to me on the plane (I told you I don't believe in luck). We struck up a conversation about the food and how surprisingly good it was. We went on to speak about the amount of traveling we both were doing. And as we spoke I realized that her schedule was far more hectic than mine. I asked how she kept up such a pace. She said she didn't mind at all because she was simply glad to be alive.

She went on to tell me that she was so excited about life because five years earlier she had been diagnosed with breast cancer, stage-three breast cancer. She was in her mid-thirties and just could not believe it was happening to her. She had no family history of breast cancer. She ate well and most of all she felt she was simply too young to have cancer. Her test results showed that the cancer had spread from the breast to the lymph nodes and the prognosis was poor. She was given two years to live, if that long. Maggie heard their predictions but she had something else that she relied on, her faith in God. She was told that she would need at least ten chemotherapy treatments and then radiation treatment. Maggie continued to think positively and continued to trust God. After five treatments, Maggie went back for her regular checkup and there was absolutely no sign of the cancer! The doctors could not believe it. Extensive tests were taken and extensive biopsies were taken but there were still no signs of cancer. Five years have come with still no sign of cancer. The cancer had totally disappeared!

Maggie is now a stage-three breast cancer survivor

who was faced with a hopeless situation. Yet she held on to her hope and faith. She never gave up. She looked death in the eye, and won. Remember that all things are possible to those who believe.

⏰ Family Faith

Doris DeBoe is also a cancer survivor, but her story of faith is quite different. She has been a friend for some time. Over the last few years she has overcome a number of illnesses, including a hernia, Parkinson's disease, and cancer. In 1983 she was diagnosed with ovarian cancer. Surgery was performed, followed by radiation treatment. Six years later it reappeared in her lungs, and then disappeared. Five years later she underwent breast surgery, again for cancer. Through it all she was not dismayed. Mrs. DeBoe said she has faith that God is in control of her life, and even though she has cancer, the cancer does not have her. She decided to enjoy life and to live every day to the fullest.

She believes that healing does not always involve a "cure" or the removal of the problem. She said that she has been healed because she has been given the strength to deal with her situation free of fear or anxiety. She believes that God didn't send the problem but He did send the grace and strength to handle it. And because of her faith she is able to have complete peace!

Her faith not only impacted her life but her faith has also impacted the lives of her friends and family members. A few years ago her brother was stricken with an abdominal aneurysm and was given less than a 5 percent chance of survival. In fact, the intensive care doctors told the family that there was nothing else that they could do for him. She started praying for her brother and helped him to develop the faith to believe that he would recover. Her faith was so strong that others found strength in her. Today her brother is back at home, living a full life and enjoying his children and grandchildren! I went to a party to celebrate his recovery and he shared how he found strength in his sister's faith and how her faith empowered the whole family. She said in order to have a miracle, you must expect a miracle. Doris DeBoe is a classic example of the power of faith. She believes that the place where the doctors end is the place where God begins. She not only believes in faith, she walks by faith! Faith is . . .

⊙ The Touch of the Master's Hand

Once upon a time there was an auction of what was considered old junk. The auctioneer came to a violin, very old and very worn and weary-looking. The auctioneer picked the violin up and plucked the strings, which were painfully out of tune. He looked at the old dirty violin, frowned and unenthusiastically started the pricing out at $10, but there were no takers. He then lowered the price to $5 but still no response. He continued to lower the price until it was going for fifty cents. He said "Fifty cents, just fifty cents. I know it's not worth much but somebody can take it for fifty cents." Right at that moment an old man with gray hair and a long gray beard walked up to the front and asked if he could hold the violin. The old man took out his handkerchief and wiped the dust and dirt off the violin. He slowly plucked the strings and meticulously tuned each string. Then he placed the old violin under his chin and began to play. And from that old violin came some of the most beautiful music that many of the people had ever heard. Beautiful songs and melodies came from that old, beat-up violin. The auctioneer then asked what was the opening price. One person said $100 and then another said $200 and then it rose and rose until it finally sold for $1,000. One thousand dollars for an old beat-up violin that no one wanted to buy for fifty cents! The story shows that little can become much when it is placed in the Master's hand!

When you place your dreams and your aspirations into the Master's hand, then you are living by faith. Faith is when you know that God Is and you are willing to accept that He Is and live like He Is! And from that assurance you can step out on the dreams that He has given you. As Les Brown says, "Faith is the assurance that you can leap and the net will appear!" Or Rosita Perez who says. "Have the faith to jump and grow wings on the way down!"

Many are not sure how faith fits into their lives, but I can say, without a question of doubt, that my faith has been my source, my guide, and my strength. For a long time I tried to do things by myself, but I failed miserably. It was only when I learned to trust God and step out on faith that I started to realize the wondrous things that could happen in my life. My constant prayer is that I will stay healthy, humble, and hungry! I pray that I stay healthy because nothing is more important or more valuable than health. If I am healthy I can do the things that can create wealth, but if I am not healthy then there would be no price that would be too high to regain good health.

Next, I pray that I will be humble. I pray for humility on a daily basis because I remember the time I thought that my successes were all my doing and I was arrogant and condescending. I had the most embarrassing performance of my life and I will never forget the important lesson I learned. I learned that I am here not to impress but rather to inspire. And just as these gifts have been freely given, they can be freely taken. I constantly pray that God will use me like a telephone, that He will speak to me and speak through me and when He is finished He will hang me up until He needs me again.

Finally, I pray that I stay hungry, that I do not become satisfied with myself, but that I will always try to better my best. The job I do tomorrow should be better than what I did today. I do not want to become complacent, but I want always to have a desire to climb the next mountain and not forget who I am and whose I am!

As my friend Larry Winget likes to say, "Faith teaches

you how to expect the best, prepare for the worst and celebrate it all!'' Celebrate life and be willing to step out on the assurance of faith! It is the Blessed Assurance that God will never leave you nor forsake you!

🕐 Footprints

One night a man had a dream. He dreamed he was walking along a beach with God. Across the sky flashed scenes from his life. For each scene he noticed two sets of footprints in the sand; one belonging to him, the other to the Lord. When the last scene of his life flashed before him, he looked back at the footprints in the sand. He noticed that many times along the paths of his life, there were only one set of footprints. He also noticed that it happened at the very lowest and saddest times in his life. This really bothered him and he questioned the Lord about it. "Lord, you said that once I decided to follow you that you'd never leave me or forsake me. You said you would walk with me all the way. But I have noticed that during the most troublesome times in my life there was only one set of footprints. I don't understand why when I needed you most you would leave me!" The Lord replied, "My precious, precious child. I love you and I would never leave you. During your time of trial and suffering, when you see only one set of footprints in the sand . . . it was then when I carried you."

AUTHOR UNKNOWN

CHAPTER IX

The Sky
Is the Limit!

The Sky Is the Limit
Lyrics by Al Johnson

You ask yourself what the future holds for you
The headline news got you scared
Like everyone else, you want peace and happiness
But is there any chance of finding it out there?
How can you forget?
The one sure thing in all of this confusion!
What you desire is already guaranteed
Promised by our Maker to all who believe!

The Sky Is the Limit
Faith can take you as far as you wanna go!
Put your heart in it
The power is yours and it's time to let it show!

You've heard it all before but it seems impossible
'Cause the world's gone completely mad!
But you don't walk alone, when the Master's in your
*   home*
He's your defense against anything that's bad
Now there will be those doubters

Telling you, you're chasing an illusion
But you know the truth and the truth will set you free
To shine as bright as any star
For the whole world to see!

The Sky Is the Limit
Faith can take you as far as you wanna go!
Put your heart in it
The power is yours and its time to let it show!

The sky truly is the limit and your faith can and will take you as far as you want to go. There will be challenges, obstacles, and difficulties that will test your resolve. But if you can have the faith and the commitment to believe and go after your dream, then you will see that it is true, The Sky Truly Is the Limit! Yet you must decide if you're willing to reach high and if so how high do you want to go.

No matter how you put it, no matter how you look at it, there is a specific bottom line in life. The bottom line is that whether you succeed or whether you fail, in the end it is up to you. When all is said and done (and usually, much more is said than done), success is a matter of choice, not chance. William Jennings Bryant stated, "Destiny is not a matter of chance, it is a matter of choice. It is not something to be waited for, but rather something to be achieved!"

⏰ Are You Still Waiting for Your Boat to Come In?

Many people speak about how they are waiting for their ship to come in. They patiently sit and wait for their break to come. I remember my days as a nightclub performer and how I was always waiting for my "Big Break," waiting to get discovered. I had always heard people say, "Just keep singing, sing real hard and one day somebody will give you a break!" I kept waiting for my break, but it never came. Then I started learning that success is a choice, not a chance. I learned that the best way to grow your future was to first grow yourself. I started a program of self-development and I decided that I was no longer going to wait for my breaks . . . I was going to make my breaks. I had a choice, I could continue to wait for my ship to come in or I could swim out to it. I decided to swim out to it, and I am so glad that I did because some of my friends are still standing at the pier, waiting. Jonathan Winters said, "I kept waiting for success, but it didn't come, so I just went on without it." Folks, success is not a thing to be waited for . . . it is a thing to be achieved! Don't just wait for your ship to come in . . . jump in and start swimming to it. You'll be glad you did!

I was speaking at a high school and a young woman waited very patiently until I had signed autographs and spoken to the other students, then she asked, "What do you do if success just won't come to you?" I responded, "Then you must *go to it*!" For a moment she seemed confused, then her eyes lit up and she said, "You mean I don't have to wait for it! Wow!"

I realized in that moment that most people have a major misconception about success. They have been miseducated. Most people believe that success is something that happens by chance and you are either lucky or not. Well, I am here to emphatically state that success does not just happen by chance but happens because we make a decision and then take action on that decision. We must decide, and then make it happen! There's an old saying that goes: "It's a funny thing about life, if you refuse to accept anything but the best, you very often get it!" That young woman left school that day with a new mind-set, she was not waiting for success to happen any longer, she was going out and making it happen.

⏰ Success Is Not a Chance, It Is a Choice!

You say you cannot choose what happens to you, so how can you choose to be successful? Well, first let's define success. Napoleon Hill, the father of success and author of *Think and Grow Rich*, defines success as the ongoing realization of a worthwhile goal or ideal. Ongoing means you are making measurable progress towards your dream. Worthwhile means that it is good and positive and helpful to our society. Hitler was not a success because his dream was wicked and evil. He was a destroyer of society rather than a builder of society. Success is an ongoing realization of a worthwhile goal or ideal. As you notice, I did not say anything about money, because we already said that success is not determined by money. There are successful mothers and fathers who have dreamed about raising honest, industrious children, and they have achieved it. Successful teachers may not be rich but have changed the lives of young people in a positive way.

But how can success be a choice? Well, it is true that there are many things in life you cannot control. But, you can control how you respond to them. You cannot control the weather or natural disasters, but you do control how you respond to them. You cannot control the economy but you do control how you respond to it. Success is not a chance, it is a choice. Rheinhold Niebuhr said, "God, give us grace to accept with serenity the things that cannot be changed, courage to change things which should be changed, and the wisdom to distinguish the one from the other." Choose to be happy, healthy, and wealthy. And remember that all things are possible if you can just believe!

It is true that we cannot determine what happens to us—the problems and circumstances that consistently challenge us. But we can determine how we react and respond to those situations. The results we get are a matter of the choices we make. And the choices we make are up to us and we must ultimately take responsibility for them. What we are and where we are is a direct result of our choices.

⏰ The Fault Is Not in the Stars

"The fault, dear Brutus, is not in our stars, but in ourselves, that we are underlings!" This is a Shakespearean quote, yet it reveals a timeless truth: We hold the key to our destiny! It is not the stars or horoscopes that will ultimately determine your destiny. It is you and your attitude to life that ultimately determines your altitude in life. I have a sign above my desk that I read daily that says it best: "Up to a point everybody's life is shaped by environment, heredity, movement, and changes in the world around them. But then there comes a time when it lies within your grasp to shape the clay of your life into the sort of thing you wish to be. Only the weak blame their parents, their race, their times, lack of good fortune, or the quirks of fate. Everyone has the power within them to say, This is what I am today and that is what I shall be tomorrow! The dream, however, must be implemented by deeds!" If it is to be, then it is up to you and me to make our dreams into realities.

⏰ Humpty Dumpty

Humpty Dumpty sat on a wall,
Humpty Dumpty had a great fall;
All the king's horses
And all the king's men
Couldn't Put Humpty Dumpty together again.
(Or wouldn't put Humpty together again.)

Whatever the case, the bottom line is that Humpty Dumpty ended up on the ground broken, busted, and totally disgusted and it was at that point that Humpty

Dumpty had to make a critical decision: to end up as a scrambled egg or sunny-side up! It doesn't matter what happens to you in life; it only matters what you do about it! Sometimes in life we are going to have problems that overwhelm us, problems that are painful, difficult, and will knock us down. We might be down, but we do not have to be out. There may be no one able or willing to help us but ourselves. That is when we must take full responsibility for ourselves. I once heard a preacher say, "You may not be responsible for getting knocked down, but you are responsible for getting back up!" I couldn't agree more. It does not matter what happens to you; it only matters what you do about it. Get up, and get busy! Remember, the choice is up to you!

Early in my speaking career I learned a great lesson about responsibility when I hired an agent to handle my bookings. I turned over all responsibility for my bookings to the agent and waited for the bookings to roll in. I waited and I waited and the phone never rang. So I fired that agent and hired another agent. Again, I waited and I waited and again the phone never rang. It finally hit me. It is their *job* to get me bookings, but it is my *responsibility*. If they do not get me bookings, then they lose that job. But if they do not get me bookings I lose my house! Whose responsibility is it? Mine! My success is ultimately up to me, and no one else.

⏱ IT'S MY RESPONSIBILITY

Hannibal said, "If you cannot find a way, then make a way!" Life is not easy and there will always be obstacles in our way. No matter what we try to achieve, there will always be obstacles. The great rewards usually have great obstacles. We must have steadfast determination to make it happen. We must decide to become the director, producer, scriptwriter, and star of our own lives. We must decide to either be distinct or to dissolve into the mainstream. George Bernard Shaw said, "People are always blaming their circumstances for what they are. I don't believe in circumstances. The people who get on in this world are the people who get up and look for the circumstances they want, and, if they can't find them, make them." We must take responsibility for our success or our failures. We must take responsibility for what we make of our lives. As stated in the poem *"Invictus"* by William Ernest Henley, "It matters not how straight the gate, how charged with punishment the scroll; I am the master of my fate; I am the captain of my soul." Ultimately it is up to you to make your dreams into realities.

⏲ The Blame Game

Excuses! Excuses! I find that I have no use for people who like to make excuses. Excuses are the tools of the incompetent, those who excel in them rarely excel in anything else! Far too often we find people who are making excuses and blaming everybody else when things go wrong. They get caught up in the "Blame Game." The "Blame Game" is a game where nobody wins, and everybody loses. It always focuses on the problem and never focuses on the solution. Losers like to play the "Blame Game," usually on a daily basis. They look for new ways to use excuses so they can continue to point the finger of blame, which has one finger pointing at others and three fingers pointing at self. They usually end up approximately at the same place they started. Winners, on the other hand, understand that in order for there to be movement someone must take responsibility. They refuse to play the "Blame Game" because they know that blame deals with the past while responsibility deals with the future. If you are going to move ahead you *must* take responsibility, which is the ability to respond. Thoreau said, "Things do not change, we change!" Do not get caught up playing the "Blame Game." Take responsibility and move on!

⏱ Leadership Is . . .

Leadership is an action, not a position! For a number of years I did programs on leadership and felt very confident with the material. A couple of years after beginning to speak on leadership I found that talking about it is one thing, but doing it is another. I became the president of the National Capital Speakers Association and found I had to actually live the things I was talking about. At the beginning of the year I took over a group that had been plagued by low membership, low attendance, and low morale. I created a twelve-point plan to double membership, attendance, revenues, and to upgrade the image of the organization and initiate some new programs. It was an ambitious concept and many of the board members questioned my sanity. First, I went about selling my vision to the board and to the membership. Second, I developed a team where everyone was involved and where everyone benefited. Finally, I shared my enthusiasm for the vision and never allowed obstacles to disrupt the plans. I am happy to say that by the end of that year, we had doubled membership, doubled attendance, and doubled revenues. We created some model programs and breathed new life into the organization! Notice I said "We." One of the first steps to leadership is to realize that it takes a team to win and everybody on the team must benefit from the success and learn from the failures. Most of all I learned that leadership is not a position . . . it is an action!

🕐 The Steps to Effective Leadership!

As I went through the year as president of the National Capital Speakers Association I learned that leadership was not a position. Leadership is an action. There were a number of steps that were necessary to develop an effective leadership team. First, you must have a vision. Then you must "sell" the vision to your teammates. You must help the team to see that the team which works together can win together; to help them to think like a team, work like a team, and then win like a team. Joe Namath said, "To be an effective leader you have to make people want to follow you; and nobody wants to follow someone who does not know where they are going!" Second, you must take action on the vision. Finally, you must take full responsibility. If things go bad, then the leader ought to be willing to take responsibility. Yet, when things are great, then the leader ought to share the credit. Leaders can and should be found at every level of the organization, from those at the top to those at the bottom. Effective leaders help to develop other leaders. The key is to remember that leadership is an action . . . not a position!

Once you accept responsibility and start the process of pursuing your dreams, there will be unplanned problems and challenges that will spring up and disrupt your progress. What do you do then? Well, those are the times when you must learn to "roll with the punches" and take the hand you are dealt and be determined to win anyway.

A few years ago I was invited to speak in Kentucky at a college convocation. I was scheduled to be at the school for approximately eighteen hours, arriving around 9 P.M. on Sunday evening and leaving the next day at 3 in the afternoon. The speech was scheduled for 10 A.M. and I got up early, expecting to be picked up about an hour before my speech. About fifteen minutes before my expected pickup, I received a call from the events coordinator and was asked if I had looked out my window. I said I had not, and when

I did I saw that the ground was covered with twelve inches of snow. During the night the area had been hit with a snowstorm and the city was shut down, including the college! All activities had been canceled, including my speech. All the roads out of the city were closed, and the governor had declared a state of emergency! The airport was closed and the roads to the airport would be closed for at least the next three days. *I was stuck!*

I looked at my schedule and found that I had a full week of speeches scheduled, and I was not going to be able to get to them. The coordinator apologized and asked if I would be okay. I told him that I was fine and there was no need to apologize. There is no need to worry or get upset about things that I cannot control. It is a waste of time and energy. I knew that I may not be able to choose what happens to me, but I can choose what I do about it and how I respond to it. And I choose to be happy, I choose to be calm and collected, and I choose to make the best out of a bad situation.

Upon realizing I was really stuck, I made some calls and rearranged my schedule. I then asked the program coordinator if someone could get me to the campus, because I had a book to finish. Those four days became a godsend, because I finally found some time to commit to this book. I got more done in those four days than I had been able to get done in months.

Statistics show that worry is a major contributor to illnesses. Worry and anxiety not only contribute to heart disease and high blood pressure but also to arthritis, rheumatism, and a lot of other illnesses. Statistics also show that married people live longer than single people, probably because they have someone to share their concerns and anxieties with, rather than having to deal with them all by themselves. Worry not only shortens your life, but it is of no use in your search for excellence. You gain nothing substantive by worrying except sickness, pain, and self-doubt. Don't worry, be happy ... because you make the choice.

If you want to be a success, then you must discard worry

and doubt and get on with your life. Each day live life with gusto and strive to be the best you can possibly be. Choose to be happy and always seek excellence in all that you do. Not perfection, but excellence. Why? Because perfection will frustrate and debilitate you, while excellence is an ongoing focus on being the best you can be. In pursuing excellence you can continue to better your best and break your personal records, without the frustration of not being perfect. We should always want to better what we did yesterday, improve what we accomplished in the past, and get stronger from each level of accomplishment.

⏰ Excellence Costs

I recently read a sign that said, "Excellence costs, you must pay the price in full; but you reap outstanding returns on your investment." There is a cost for excellence. It is not cheap, but the returns are outstanding because they continue to bring dividends. Excellence is like truth; no matter how much you push it down and try to cover it up, it will always rise to the top. It cannot be denied. It is like the phoenix that rises from the ashes; no matter how you try to destroy and disrupt it, excellence will always rise from the ashes. Life is difficult for everyone; the rain falls on the righteous as well as the unrighteous, but those who believe in excellence and pursue it with passion are those who are not overcome by the vicissitudes of life. Don't just *go* through the problems and challenges but rather *grow* through them. Excellence costs . . . but pays outstanding rewards!

You must dream, then make a conscious determined decision and take action, and, finally, strive for excellence in your pursuit. Yet a lack of real desire causes many to give up and never reach their potential. Desire is the element that separates the achievers from the mere dreamers. Desire is the element that some call "the little extra that makes the big difference." You've got to want to be a success and you've got to want to be excellent. You've got to want to make your dreams into realities and you've got to want to achieve greatness. You've got to want it and want it bad!

I was speaking at a high school some years ago and I met a young man who was about six-foot-five and two hundred and fifty pounds, and all muscle. He looked like Charles Atlas; he was a perfect physical specimen. After the program I asked him what he wanted to be and he told me that he wanted to play professional football. I told him that he definitely had the physique, but I wondered if he had the desire, since the professional sports field is very competitive. He said he wanted it badly. I said, "How bad?" and he said, "Real bad." I said, "Real bad?" and he replied, "Real bad." Then I asked him the definitive question: "Do you want it badly enough to go through a brick wall?" and he replied, "No, I don't want it *that* bad." I said, "My friend, until you want it badly enough to go through a brick wall, it will be extremely difficult for you to achieve success and reach the professional level. Mere talent is still not enough, you must want it bad!" There are million of people with great talents who are not using their talents but are working jobs that they settled for because the competition was too tough and they didn't want to achieve their dreams badly enough. They did not have that little bit of extra "oomph" to rise above the masses. They didn't have the desire.

You've got to want it so badly that you are willing to go through a brick wall. You may never have to go through that brick wall but you must be willing, if necessary. To be a success at any level, you must want it bad! The great football coach Vince Lombardi said, "The difference between a successful person and others is not a lack of strength, not a lack of knowledge, but rather in a lack of will." DESIRE!

⏱ How Badly Do You Want It?

"So you want to be a rock star, huh?" That was a question a record company executive asked me when I walked into his office years ago. And he then asked me if I was willing to do what it takes to be a rock star. Was I willing to leave the comforts of home? Was I willing to move to another city? Was I willing to live on the streets until I made it? Was I willing to get up early and stay up late? Was I willing to do whatever it takes? He said that I might not have to pay that price, but I have to be willing. Well, most people are not willing to give their all to be a rock star, a doctor star, a nurse star, a computer star, a sales star, an architect star, an entrepreneur star, or any other kind of star—because you have to be willing to give your all if you want your dreams to come true.

Do you want it bad? Are you serious? I mean real serious? As the saying goes, "Are you as serious as a heart attack?" Because a heart attack will take you out, it does not play! Are you really serious about your success? Are you willing to go the extra mile, to do the little extra that makes the big difference? Are you willing to stay up late and get up early? Are you willing to turn off the TV and read books that will help you to better yourself? Are you willing to experience some pain and rejection as your pursue your dream? Are you willing to do that which is uncomfortable? Are you willing to fight for your dreams? Are you serious? Are you serious about what you're doing or are you just dabbling?

Many people really think they are serious, but in reality they are just going through the motions. They think they are being serious, but in reality they are just fooling themselves. They are active and busy but they are not going anywhere. It's like they're running on a treadmill, running fast and going nowhere. A lot of people fool themselves and do not realize the difference between activity and results. How do I know? Because I was one of those people who was busy but going nowhere. For years I was a whirl-wind of activity, but when I looked closely I realized I hadn't accomplished anything. I was going through the motions, but I wasn't really serious. I didn't want it badly enough.

When you are serious, you are willing to go the extra mile and give the extra little bit. You are willing to do that which is uncomfortable. Your level of commitment rises to another level. You look for ways to constantly improve your best effort. You dig in, and make a decision to become steadfast, unmovable, and unstoppable, no matter what it takes!

Ask yourself the question, "What would I do, if I were serious?" What goals would I pursue? What things would I continue to do and what actions would I stop? What nonproductive, time-wasting activities would I eliminate? What would I do if I were really serious? Ask yourself the question and your mind will give you the answer. Once you get the answers, take a sheet of paper and write them down. Read them and start to work on the list. No matter what you are presently doing, you can do more. You can always accomplish and achieve more, if you willing to get serious.

Friends, pursue excellence in all that you do. Develop great desire and commitment to reach your goals and then take full responsibility for your success. Get serious, and in short order you will start to see your dreams begin to sprout, grow, and bloom.

⏱ Dare Greatly

Theodore Roosevelt believed that life is for the living and if you are going to live you might as well go big, or not at all. You are either on the way or in the way, either a spectator of life or a valiant participant in life. The following quote shares why Teddy Roosevelt was able to become a legend in his own time. It expresses

his commitment to live life to the fullest. It is called "Dare Greatly" and that is what he encourages us to do . . . Dare Greatly! "It is not the critic who counts; nor the man who points out how the strong stumbled, or where the doer of the deed could have done better. The credit belongs to the man who is actually in the arena; whose face is marred by dust and sweat and blood; who strives valiantly; who errs and comes up short again and again. Who knows the great enthusiasms, the great devotions, and spends himself in a worthy cause; who at the best knows in the end the triumphs of high achievement; and who at the worst, if he fails, at least fails while daring greatly; so that his place shall never be with those cold and timid souls who know neither victory or defeat." Live life to the fullest!

I encourage you to recognize that life is a gift that should be appreciated and enjoyed to the utmost. Do not end up a spectator in the stands. Make a decision to get on the field and participate. This is another quote that I keep above my desk: "Seats on the 50-yard line are nice, but they do not interest me, because I am here to play and I plan to WIN!"

⏰ Simple Rules for Life

Successful living does not have to be a complicated process. Someone said that success in life is simple; it is not easy, but it is simple. I read a book that stated everything we really need to know we learned in kindergarten! I am not sure if everything we need to know we learned there, but I do believe that many of the most important things we need to know we learned in kindergarten. Success is simple, not easy, but simple. These are a few of the simple rules for life:

1. Take time to dream (remember, most great achievements were once considered impossible).
2. Think often and deeply.

3. Treat others the way you would like to be treated.
4. Say thank you and please, a lot!
5. Greet each day with a smile.
6. Never argue with an idiot; those who are watching will not be able to tell the difference (never wrestle with a pig; you'll both get dirty and the pig likes it).
7. Choose to be happy.
8. Make a commitment to excellence (remember, if you do the things today that others won't do, you'll have the things tomorrow that others won't have).
9. Be grateful (remember, if there were no problems there would be no opportunities).
10. Love life! Have fun! Never underestimate the power, potential, and possibilities of the human spirit. Life really is a blast!

It really is not complicated; unfortunately, many make it complicated. Scott Skiles said, "Life is a lot like going to church, many attend . . . but few understand." Have faith, believe, and remember that the sky truly is the limit! Always reach for the sky and if you miss you will be among the stars!

CHAPTER X

Small Steps
Taken on a
Mighty Long Road

Midnight Phoenix
Lyrics by Diane Kenney
From the play "Skegee" by Deborah Sims-Wood

A Midnight Phoenix rises
From the ashes of the past
Shimmering in the darkness
It spreads its wings at last

A golden sun illuminates
The grassy plains below
And crimson blossoms bloom again
Where nothing used to grow

Small Steps taken on a mighty long road
Small Steps taken on a mighty long road
Small Steps taken on a mighty long road

The music of the universe
Still echoes in the song
Of nightingales and hummingbirds
Why can't we sing along?

WILLIE JOLLEY

Discordant notes will sound again
Unless we understand
And the primal memory once awake
Creates its own demand

Small Steps taken on a mighty long road
Small Steps taken on a mighty long road
Small Steps taken on a mighty long road

So you lift your voice I'll lift mine
Let harmony restore, our faith in dreams
Brotherhood and peace for evermore

Small steps taken on a mighty long road
Small steps taken on a mighty long road
Small steps taken on a mighty long road

It's a Mighty Long Road, But We're Gonna Make It!

It sometimes seems like an endless road, but everything ends, even hard times and adversity. And out of the darkness of our tragedies and adversity can come the seeds for a complete turnaround and transformation. Just like the phoenix rises from the ashes, the first steps may seem so small, yet those small steps lead to great rewards. In those moments of difficulty are born many of the wonderful triumphs and turnarounds. Dennis Kimbro likes to say that a setback is a setup for a comeback! Those small moments of personal decision to face adversity and to go on in spite of the pain and discomfort lead to hours of victory and accomplishment.

⏰ The Chicken and the Eagle!

Once upon a time there was an eagle's nest that sat on the top of the highest mountain peak. A strong wind came and blew an egg out of the nest and and it rolled down the mountain into a valley and ended up in a

chicken farm. The mother hen saw the little eagle egg and said, "What a funny-looking chicken egg, but I'll sit on it and make it my little chicken!" The mother hen sat on the egg until it hatched. When it hatched out came this big beak and big feet and huge wings. The mother looked at the little bird and said, "What a funny-looking chicken, but you can be one of my little chickens." And even though that bird was born with eagle genes and eagle chromosomes, it was born in chicken surroundings. So it thought it was a chicken. It walked like a chicken and it talked like a chicken. It thought like a chicken and it dreamed like a chicken. Its biggest chicken dream was to one day get on top of the fence, so it could crow like a rooster. It figured if it could only do that then the other birds wouldn't laugh and make fun of the fact that it looked different. But each time it dreamed that dream, it would say to itself, "You know you can never get on top of that fence! You know they always told you that chickens can't fly!" So it didn't even try. It would just give up and walk away. One day while standing out in the barnyard, the little bird looked up and saw the most magnificent sight it had ever seen. It saw the sight of an eagle flying majestically across the sky, like the king of the sky. The little bird was so amazed that it shouted with all that was within, "What are you? What are you?" The big eagle, with its powerful hearing and powerful eyesight, saw the little bird and flew straight down and said, "What am I? What are you?" and the little bird said, "I'm a chicken." The big eagle looked the little bird straight in the eye and said, "Look at my face, you look just like me! Look at my beak, you look just like me! Look at my wings, you look just like me! Friend, you are not a chicken, you are an eagle! Flap your wings and fly like the eagle you were born to be. The little bird flapped his wings . . . and he flew, and he soared above the clouds! Friends, you were not born to be chickens, you were born to be eagles. Fly like the eagles you were born to be!

Whitney Houston sang a wonderful song called "One Moment In Time," which is about the importance of one moment. It details how one moment, one defining moment, can change your life. In that moment you recognize that each day is a brand-new opportunity to give your best and you can face the future with optimistic anticipation and excited expectancy. This is one moment, one defining moment in which you realize that you are a winner who must seize that moment and go forth into the future with enthusiasm because you know that moment is the moment for which you have been prepared. Go forth and be mindful that there will be challenges, knowing with the ups there will be some downs, with the sweet there will be some sour, with joy there will be some pain, yet in those moments when you are by yourself, you will know that you are never alone.

One moment in time! In everybody's life, there are those moments that define the direction and context of our lives. Those moments are commonly called "defining moments" and are those brief moments, those tiny minutes that alter our lives and thereby alter the lives of others. Rosa Parks had a defining moment one day in 1955 in Montgomery, Alabama, when she refused to give up her seat on a bus, because she was tired. She made a decision at that moment that would spark a movement that ultimately changed this country. During the desperate search for someone to lead the Montgomery people in a bus boycott, a twenty-six-year-old preacher said, "I'll do it," and the world would never be the same because Martin Luther King, Jr., made a decision that would change his destiny. It was a defining moment when the apostle Paul had an encounter on the Damascus road that changed his life and changed the world. In a moment he went from being a persecutor of the Christians to the greatest defender of the faith. It happened in just a moment. It was also a defining moment when the thief we spoke of earlier was hanging on a cross next to Jesus and realized that he could change his life if he would just say, "Remember me, when you come into your kingdom."

We all have defining moments in our lives, moments that change the emphasis of our existence. Some would say that our destiny is determined in those moments. However, many of us back off or shy away from those moments, because they are uncomfortable. Defining moments are by their nature uncomfortable, but growth is uncomfortable. Change is uncomfortable, yet it is a daily part of life. Those defining moments are the moments that create winners.

We all have defining moments that have altered and affected our direction, but it only becomes a defining moment when it actually defines and shapes our characters and perspectives. It is really not the moment that defines it, but our response to the moment that makes the difference. We all have moments that are unexpected and that alter our histories, but many run from those moments and wilt in the heat of those moments. They refuse to rise to the challenges of the moment.

Franklin Delano Roosevelt had a defining moment the day he woke up and discovered his legs wouldn't move because he had been stricken by polio. Yet he made the decision to keep going after his dream. He went on to become one of the most popular presidents in this nation's history and the only president ever elected four times!

Winston Churchill had a defining moment when as a child his classmates were teasing and berating him because of his severe stuttering problem. He made up his mind he would prove to the world that he had something to say and would say it! He overcame his stuttering and became a gifted orator. And because of those skills, he became a national leader and eventually the prime minister of England. He went on to be awarded a Nobel Peace Prize and become one of the most quoted speakers of all time.

⏱ Dennis Byrd

In 1992, Dennis Byrd was a very popular defensive lineman for the New York Jets. On one Sunday he was involved in a freak accident with one of his teammates

and at that moment his life was forever changed. He remained on the ground after the collision with his teammate and was unable to move his hands or feet. The doctors and team trainers ran on the field. Byrd told them that he had no feeling from his neck down. Initially they thought it was a "stinger," which is a condition that temporarily deadens the nerves. But after a few days they realized that this was not a temporary condition and that Dennis Byrd was in fact paralyzed for life. The doctors gave him a battery of tests and concluded that he would never walk again, but Dennis Byrd was not a typical patient and didn't accept those conditions. Dennis Byrd had overcome obstacles just to get the opportunity to play professional football, after he had been told that he would never be good enough. He had something that was greater than any obstacle that he would face—his great faith in God and in himself.

In all of the interviews, while he was still in the hospital, he continued to say that his faith would bring him through. He never gave up that belief! Today he is the president of the Dennis Byrd Foundation. In the fall of 1993, Dennis Byrd was honored by the New York Jets for his courage and commitment to excellence. On that day Dennis Byrd returned to the same field where he had experienced his defining moment and had been paralyzed. On that day Dennis Byrd walked onto that field under his own strength without a cane or a walker. He was empowered by his great faith and great determination. Faith is the key. Believe and receive.

Dr. Robert Schuller shared one of his defining moments and how it changed his life and his ministry. He told how in 1953 he had gone to California to start a church and was led to use the only place he could find, a drive-in theater. He started and planned to only use that location until he could save enough money to get a chapel. He began the church and because of the unique nature of the church he got some unique members, like Ms. Rosie, who couldn't attend regular churches because they were not equipped for handicapped members. Ms. Rosie attended the church and became an important part of the church.

Finally, Reverend Schuller was ready to move to his chapel, but what would he do with Ms. Rosie. He was faced with a tough decision: open the new chapel or stay at the drive-in and limit his growth. It was at that instant that he had a defining moment. He realized that his mission was to serve and he couldn't limit nor exclude people in his service. He choose to expand to the new chapel but also to continue the drive-in service, and to make plans to build a new church that was a combination church and drive-in worship center.

He went on to purchase the land for a new church and in that quest he had to cash in his life insurance, mortgage his home, sell his car, and borrow to the limit. The result is the Crystal Cathedral and Dr. Schuller's Hour of Power, which is a worldwide ministry that has changed the lives of countless millions. Dr. Schuller experienced a defining moment that changed his life and changed the lives of others; a moment defined because of a small handicapped woman named Ms. Rosie.

Nathan Hale had a defining moments that changed and charged a movement. During the Revolutionary War Nathan Hale volunteered for a very dangerous mission behind enemy lines. While on his way back from the mission, he was captured and sentenced to death within twenty-four hours. He was not allowed any communication with others and his handwritten note to his parents was torn up in front of his eyes. Yet at the moment of the ascent up the stairs he made a statement that changed the whole mood of the war effort, ''I only regret that I have only one life to lose for my country.'' He was only twenty-one years old but he had a courage and calmness of mind that was beyond his years. At that moment he sparked a rally that inspired the revolutionary forces and pushed them on to win despite the odds, and has continued to inspire countless generations of Americans since.

One of my defining moments was the moment I went

from being a good, but limited local performer to planting the seed to be a performer who had the potential for greatness. I was invited to perform at a showcase in Nashville, Tennessee, and I went with the attitude that I was God's gift to the music industry. I went with the mind-set that I would dazzle them with my showmanship and not worry about the actual singing. Well, it was a complete disaster! I was a complete flop, a complete dud! The walk from that stage that night was the loneliest walk I had ever had in my life. I was used to the crowds cheering and now I was getting nothing but silence. I realized at that moment that the problem was not my talent but rather how I had chosen to use my talents. I had tried to simply impress and share nothing of any substance, when I should have tried to entertain to inspire and make others feel better. I was merely going through the motions. My performance had no passion and no purpose. I decided in that moment I would not take my talents nor my audiences for granted ever again. That was a defining moment that established the seed for greater possibilities in my future. Napoleon Hill said that in every adversity are the seeds for an equal or greater opportunity. I know for sure that that statement is true!

One of the most important moments that helped define my life happened on a sunny October day in 1970. I rushed home from school to change clothes for an evening baseball game and ran into the house to find my father on the floor unconscious. He was not breathing and was unresponsive to my calls. I called 911 and calmly told the operator that my father was lying on the floor unconscious. Then I called my mother at work and told her that she should come home because Dad was not well. I did not want to frighten her, even though I was well aware of the situation. When my mother arrived home the paramedics had taken the body away and I had to comfort my mother and then tell my brother that Dad had died. That day I went from being a boy to being a man.

Defining moments! Those moments that can define us or deflate us, make us or break us, help us or hurt us, create us or conquer us. It all depends on how we respond to the moment that makes the difference and that shapes our destiny. If we grasp the moment and grow through it, not just go through it but grow through it, we become stronger. If we wilt under the pressure and give up on the moment, we tend to become weaker. An old proverb states that the same hammer that molds the steel shatters the glass. Defining moments are unpredictable, yet they have a profound effect on our futures.

⏰ "If" (by Rudyard Kipling)

If you can keep your head when all about you
Are losing theirs and blaming it on you,
If you can trust yourself when all men doubt you,
But make allowances for their doubting too;
If you can wait and not be tired by waiting,
Or being lied about, don't deal in lies,
Or being hated, don't give away to hating,
And yet don't look too good, nor talk too wise:

If you can dream and not make dreams your
    master;
If you can think and not make thoughts your aim;
If you can meet triumph and disaster
And treat those two impostors just the same;
If you can bear to hear the truth you've spoken
Twisted by knaves to make a trap for fools,
Or watch the things you gave your life to, broken,
And stoop and build 'em up with worn out tools:
If you can make one heap of all your winnings
And risk it on one turn of pitch-and-toss,
And lose, and start again at your beginnings
And never breathe a word about your loss;
If you can force your heart and nerve and sinew
To serve your turn long after they are gone,
And so hold on when there is nothing in you
Except "The Will" which says to them, "Hold
    On!"

If you can talk crowds and keep your virtue,
Or walk with kings, nor lose the common touch,
If neither foes not loving friends can hurt you,
If all men count with you, but none too much;
If you can fill the unforgiving minute
With sixty seconds worth of distance run,
Yours is the earth and everything that's in it,
And, which is more, you'll be a man, my son!

⏱ Hold Your Ground

When I was a child I remember playing a game called "Uncle," where someone would play hide-and-seek and when you were found they would all hold you down and tickle you until you said "Uncle" and gave up. Some of our playmates would easily give up and say "Uncle," but there was another group who refused to say "Uncle." No matter what you did to them, they would not say "Uncle." In time, I realized that those were the same people who tended to be the leaders and the most respected by the other kids.

I learned that when you hold your ground and refuse to give in to the pressure, it is going to be difficult and uncomfortable. Yet those who hold on and stand their ground are the ones who tend to have the highest respect levels. Nelson Mandela refused to compromise and give in. During his twentieth year in jail, the South African government offered him his freedom, if he agreed to compromise and accept Apartheid. He had to make a decision that he knew would impact his life. He was getting old and his time was running out to see his children and spend time with his family. Prison life was extremely hard and cruel. But he chose to stay in prison and not give in! He held his ground and his stature grew not only among the people in South Africa but also among those in other countries.

As you move among your daily pursuits there will be some days when you will find yourself being asked to give up, give in, and say "Uncle." The pressure will be strong and the road will be difficult, but remember someone is always looking at you, and looking to you to provide leadership. Don't give in. Don't wilt under the pressure. Hold your ground and you will grow from the experience, not only in the way others see you, but, more importantly, in the way you see yourself. Remember all things are possible if you can just believe!

I remember as a young man that the more things change, the more they stay the same. When I was about 14 years old and was in the youth choir of Asbury United Methodist Church in Washington, D.C., we performed a piece of music called "Desiderata," which totally intrigued me. I was amazed at how hip and cool the writer was and how much he had a pulse on the world of today. Then I found out that it wasn't written this century or last century or even the one before that. I was amazed when I found out that this piece was written over five hundred years ago. I realized that it is true, that the more things change the more they stay the same!

⏰ Desiderata

Go placidly amid the noise and haste. And remember what peace there may be in silence. And as far as possible without surrender, be on good terms with all persons. Speak your truth quietly and clearly and listen to others, even the dull and ignorant, they too have their stories. Avoid loud and aggressive people, they are vexations to the spirit. If you compare yourself with others you may become vain and bitter. For always there will be greater and lesser persons than yourself. Enjoy your achievements, as well as your plans. Keep interested in your own career, however humble. It is a real possession in the changing fortunes of time. Exercise caution in your business affairs, for the world is full of trickery. Let this not blind you to what virtue there is. Many persons strive for high ideals and everywhere life is full of heroism. Be yourself, especially do not feign affection, neither be cynical about love. In the face of all aridity and disenchantment, it is perennial as the grass. Take kindly the counsel of the years, gracefully surrendering the things of youth. Nurture strength of spirit to shield you in sudden misfortunes. But do not distress yourself with imaginings. Many fears are born of fatigue and loneliest beyond a wholesome discipline, be gentle with yourself. You are a child of the universe, no less than the trees and the stars, you have a right to be here, and whether or not it is clear to you, no doubt the universe is unfolding as it should. Therefore, be at peace with God. And whatever your labors and aspirations, and the noisy confusion of life. Keep peace with your soul. With all its sham, drudgery and broken dreams, strive to be happy!

⏰ Bright Moments

Years ago I had the opportunity to meet a traveling musician who had an impact on, me even though I only had a few opportunities to talk to him. I didn't get to know him well; in fact, I don't even know his real name, except that everyone called him "Bright Moments." The reason they called him that was because he would always greet you by saying "Bright Moments" rather than hello, and he would leave with the same statement, rather than saying good-bye. He was a very peaceful yet powerful presence; he looked in your eyes and shook your hand with genuine and sincere interest. I was young and was impressed by this guy and learned how to greet and appreciate each person I had the opportunity to meet because each person is special in the sight of God. Just from those brief moments with him I was able to learn, firsthand, about treating others as I really wanted to be treated. As quickly as he came, he left and I never saw him again, but I will always remember the lessons I learned. **Love life, live as you would like to be treated, always be thankful, enthusiastic, and excited about life. And always share positive greetings, and salutations with others, because as you water the plants of others you cannot help but get some water on yourself!**

I send you forth to follow your dream and then go after it with all that you have within you. And I bid that you will be "Blessed and Highly Favored" and always have "Bright Moments" every day of your life.

Ladies and gentlemen, as I end this book I want to remind you that you have greatness and unlimited power within you. Always dream the big dream, think the big thought, and treat others as you would like to be treated because we are all independent, yet interdependent and interrelated. We can make a difference! We can change the world, but first we must change ourselves!

"*It Only Takes a Minute to Change Your Life!*" The minute you make the decision to change and take action is the minute you change your life. The skirmishes will come but the battle will be won!

⏱ **Stay Motivated! Highly Motivated! And really live your dreams!**

Highly Motivated
(by Willie Jolley)

I had a job, a job I really hated
It made me sick, but it got me motivated
I knew that this was not
Where I was meant to be
I didn't want to stay
But I was too afraid to leave

But then one day I got my check
And there was almost nothing there

I went to the boss
He laughed and said he didn't care
My kids were at home hungry
I was about to lose my home
That's when I decided I had to make it on my own

I'm Motivated, Highly Motivated, I'm Motivated,
Gonna Take It to the Top
I'm Motivated, Highly Motivated, I'm Motivated
I'm Never Gonna Stop

My friends said I was crazy
When I told them all good-bye
But the only one who's crazy
Is the one who's afraid to try
They said I'd never make it
Said I would not survive
But I knew I had to make it
It was either do or die

So I grabbed hold of my dream
and I put it in my heart
I stepped out on my faith
and I learned to really trust in God
I knew I had to fight
fight with all my power
Then things started happening
Blessings came, oh, hour after hour

So I'm Motivated, Highly Motivated, I'm Motivated
Gonna Take It to the Top
I'm Motivated, Highly Motivated, I'm Motivated
I'm never gonna stop!

Hannibal said, "If you cannot find a way, then make a
way"
It doesn't matter so much what happens around you, or
to you
What matters is what happens in you!

When people stomp on your dreams
Don't get mad, don't get even . . . Get Ahead!
Because massive success IS the best revenge!

So when people laugh at you
And they try to put you down
Take that negative
And then turn it all around
Grab hold of your dreams
Let it set your soul on fire
Activate your faith
And take it higher and higher

If you've the faith, God's got the power
To bless your life, hour after hour
Keep the faith
Keep the desire, keep reaching up
Until you reach the . . . Sky!

REMEMBER THAT ALL THINGS ARE POSSIBLE IF YOU CAN JUST BELIEVE!
This is Willie Jolley. Have a Fantastic Day!
ALWAYS DREAM THE IMPOSSIBLE DREAM!

For more information on Willie Jolley and his motivational programs, products and services, contact:
http://www.williejolley.com
or
The Motivational Minute Hotline
888-2-MOTIV8
(888-266-8488)